Through the Eyes of the Enemy

Memoirs of a German SS Artillery Man and British POW

Manfred Gutzke

TRAVELOGUE 219

Through the Eyes of the Enemy

TL219-316, 'Through the Eyes of the Enemy' February 2018
Edition 1.1
Published by: Travelogue 219
Toronto, Canada
www.tl219.com

ISBN 978-1-927679-59-3

Front cover by Luigi A. Cannavicci

Contents

Editor's note: there were no chapter titles in Manfred's original manuscript and have been added by John Sliz. Roy and Patty Gutzke and John came up with the titles for the parts.

Author Forward

This life story was written down in the year 1977, Toronto Canada, upon the urging of my son Roy, who was born in Toronto Nov. 1955. It is just an ordinary life, with no favours from anyone in the turmoil of the times in Germany (1927 to 1954). To Hell and Back .... I made it.

Manfred Gutzke

Forward by Fred Schmidt

Back in the very late 1970s or very early 1980s, I met Manfred's son Roy and we became good friends. Not long after that, I met Manfred himself. Little did I know at this time, that Manfred Gutzke was busy writing his memoirs of the war as per Roy's request. He wrote part of it in 1977 and part of it in 1980. When complete, the documents were bound up with a note that they were not to be opened until his death. I think I saw the sealed package once while Manfred was still alive. Roy and I had both heard bits and pieces of his experiences in WWII. However, knowing that he had written hundreds of pages, and the fact that he did not want it read while he was alive, made it clear to us that there were some amazing stories in those notes. To say we were not disappointed is an understatement. Even though Manfred's accent was thick and his English grammar was poor, he hand wrote the notes in English, which truly highlighted his acceptance of Canada as his new home and new identity. It was clear that he wanted to leave the land where he had experienced all those atrocities behind and start over as a Canadian.

During the decades that I knew Manfred, I knew he used to be a German soldier in WWII and that he had incredible experiences. I did not know for quite some time that he was an SS soldier and before that he was in the Hitler youth. I also did not know that he spent many of his war years on the front lines fighting the Russians, or that he was one of the first to have witnessed new war technology such as the V2. Manfred was careful about what bits of information he shared with me regarding his incredible past. I also knew not to ask too much more. I felt a kinship to Manfred and Roy because I am also a Canadian-born son of German parents who had to endure the horrors of WWII. I also had an Oma who struggled through both WWI and WWII in Germany. I spent my childhood listening to tales of those bad times. Thankfully, my parents were younger than Manfred and my father was too young to be conscripted. My grandfather, however, was not so lucky and died on the front lines in France in 1940, unable to tell me his tales as Manfred was able to tell Roy.

Manfred was a very tall man, spoke with authority, was pragmatic and practical, independent and resourceful, and a no-nonsense type of guy who still enjoyed a good joke and had an occasionally warped sense of humour. These are all qualities that would have been required to survive the horrors he endured during WWII. He was also sometimes cranky and short tempered. The reasons for that will become apparent after reading the book. Additionally he suffered from significant hearing loss from all of that action during the war. Even as he approached his final years, he still had habits from the war years of re-using and repurposing items, and also creating useful items and works of art from what many of us might consider junk. He was very good at it. If he did not have those skills, he likely would have not survived the war.

Manfred Gutzke passed away in 2013. It took a while before his son Roy started to dig into Manfred's sealed notes. Fascinating stories emerged, and we knew how important these were but they sat on a shelf for a number of years because we didn't know how to move forward. Fast forward to 2016 when I met author and publisher John Sliz. We both realized we had love of history and not long afterward I told him about Manfred's notes and introduced him to Roy. We all got excited and worked as a team to organize Manfred's notes and bring his incredible stories to life where they could be enjoyed by all. Manfred's notes managed to capture not only important historical events, but he was also able to convey the minute details that some historians miss and he was able to capture the emotions and feelings of himself, his community and his country during those years. He takes you from his early years where he was admittedly duped by the propaganda of the Nazi Regime, to later realizing what it really was and then to a literal battle of survival towards the end of the war. He witnessed the rise and fall of an empire from the most brutal of angles. Most of his classmates did not survive. He was lucky, indeed.

Roy, kudos to you for encouraging your father to record his insightful, historic and fantastic stories.

To quote Manfred exactly from his notes: "Roy, this is good to read and to heed. Times like that I do not wish on anyone. Let's hope they never come again anyplace. Be glad you did not have to go through such times." We all agree with you Manfred and were glad you made it out of there alive to start over and live your life to a respectable age!

Fred Schmidt

Through the Eyes of the Enemy

Part I: Youth to Manhood to Wartime SS

Chapter One:

I am Manfred Max George Gutzke

My parents, Max-Karl-Otto Gutzke and Martha-Ruth-Maria Pehlke, were married in 1921 in Roggow, Germany, which is now called Rogowo in Poland. The Village got its name from an old house on the road to the city. Father* was born in the next village in March 1987. My mother was from the same village and was born in January 1896.

During their first years together my parents lived in the house of my grandmother, Berta Pehlke, in Roggow, where they had only one room with a kitchen. The house was built very likely in the late 1700s. These were Colonist houses from the time of Prussian king Fredrick the Great and had old thatch roof clay and wood walls still attached to the house with a hayloft over the rooms.

My sister, Charlotte, was born in December 1921.

As it was told to me, one Sunday my parents went for a walk across the Persante River where they saw that some new houses

* Where my father came from: my sister - after some research in church records - never found out. She was able to trace our ancestors on our mother's side back to more or less 1812 in this same area, a 15KM circle, all in the church records.

were being built on a street 4km from Roggow. After some questions they found out that they were eligible to build there too, mostly because my father was a bricklayer. They applied for a government loan of 12,000 Reichsmark, for which they got the house and the land. The lot was 60 meters by 150 meters. In 1925 my father started the house in STERNKRUG, a place 16 degrees east of Greenwich where it intercepts 54 degrees latitude. It was an inn called the Krugzum Goldenen Stern or the Inn to the Golden Star. The village was then named Sternkrug (Star Inn). Sternkrug was a nice village, only 4km from the city of Belgard, which had a population of 15,000 and was a very old city with the gate and part of an old defense wall still standing. It was in the eastern part of Pomerania. Belgard means Blue

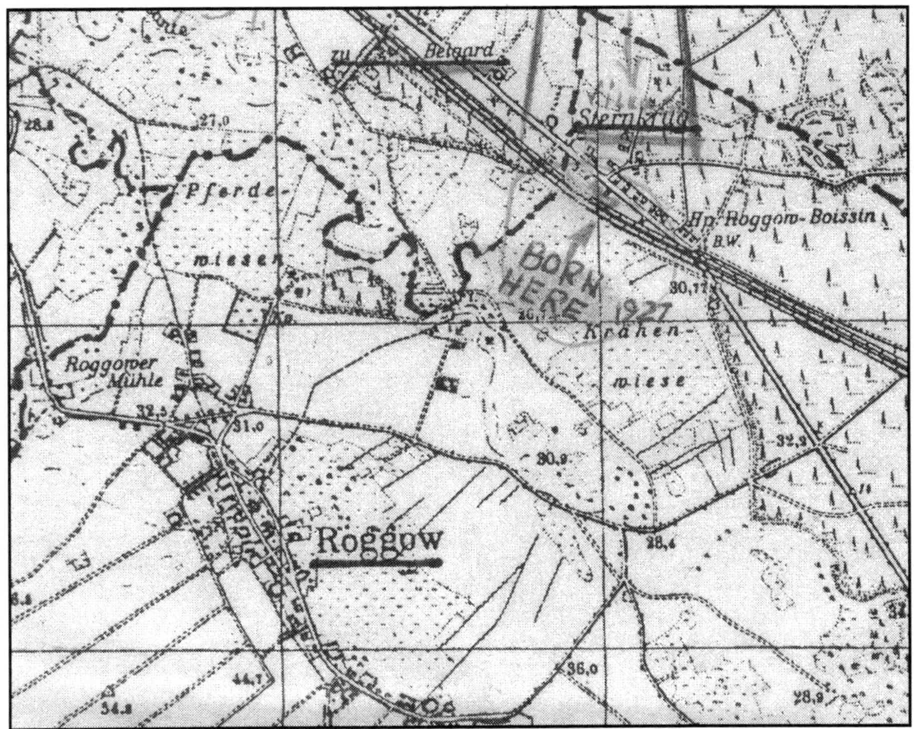

Above: a map drawn on by Manfred showing where he was born in 1927. (Roy Gutzke Collection)

Castle. There was also a Naugard & Stargrard, grey and white, castle.

It was very hard going. The top floor was not completely finished until mother found a good friend in a local farmer in the village. The farmer had owned all the land where the houses were built in Sternkrug and he gave mother the lumber to finish the house. My mother and his wife became lifelong friends. After completion it had to stand empty in 1926 because it was the rule that the house had to dry out for a year.

The final mortgage payment for the house was made by my sister in 1944.

St. Patrick's Day 1927 (17th of March) I was born in the house that my father had built. My Christian name is Manfred because my mother liked the name from the Red Baron, Manfred von Richthofen. One day I asked my mother where she got my name from. As she was very religious she was going to name me Johannes. Father did not like this name. Then Hertha Kath came by one day with the name Manfred. She heard it in school discussing Richthofen, The Red Baron.

My second name, Max was the first name of my father. The third name, George, was very fashionable at this time. It was the name from the King of England. All boys had George in their names. Everything was solved with names. Father, like Manfred and I, was christened that way in our house as my mother was very religious. She got the priest from the city for the service and other children were christened in our house as well.

In the years before school I remember that I went in a car one time to a place called Elfenbusch to visit my uncle. Here we crossed a ditch with water and I was told this was the Persante River, a few feet wide at best. This came by our village at 100 km down river and by that time it was quite a clear stream. In the summertime it was very good to swim and just have fun. This is where I learned how to swim. We had to cross this river on our way to school every day – in summer 7am to noon – in winter 8 to 1 or 5 hours a day. Sometimes in the spring the river overflowed and took the bridge out. The bridge was called Crows-bridge and was located in a bushy area, nesting grounds for a large colony of crows in the trees.

I can truly say I surely enjoyed the time I had before school with my father. He was home in the winter or worked in the bush at times. Once he told me to come and visit him in the bush and he would show me where the Hexen (witch) House was. He sure did

Above: the house that Manfred's father built. Photo taken in 1992 by Manfred's sister Charlotte. Manfred planted the two trees in front of the house in 1938. (Roy Gutzke Collection)

so and the sight of the House of a Hex scared the daylight out of me. It had a straw roof. Father, being taller than me, saw the whole house through the trees, not realizing I was only seeing the roof. Later I found out it was a feeding station for wildlife, built by the game warden. But while I was a little boy I always knew where the Hex was in the bush. He also showed me the tracks of deer and foxes. I learned to read all sorts of tracks of wild animals in the snow. The snow was quite deep every winter and on a cold day it would squeak under your shoes.

My father also showed me how to do some work at home. I didn't have to work hard though, just make enough firewood for mother for the day and double the load on Saturday. There was no wood splitting at our house on a Sunday. Mother was very religious and wouldn't allow me to split wood on Sunday. On top of the stall was a hayloft where mother had placed 3 long benches. She had convinced the pastor from the city to hold prayers at our house several times a year. I hated this routine as it was work getting ready for it and my Sunday was spoiled. When the house was built Mother had insisted that Father put in an extra door. He put the door in not knowing the reason for it. Later he found this was the entrance for church into their living room. People didn't have to go through the kitchen. Mother was always late getting ready on the day of the Church Service and was rushing in the kitchen washing up. I hated to go to people and tell them there was church at our house on Sunday. The women all came as they did not dare to offend Mother. She let it be known who had not attended.

In the long winter evenings I talked a lot with my mother and she told me in the mid 1930's that one day man would go to the moon around year 2000 and I would be there to see it.

Mother liked the better things in life. This very modern village had an unusual population. There were several people from Bolshevik Russia, as it was called then. The people had fled after the Bolshevik revolution and the German government had taken them in. They had been given the same money, and like others, built their house in Sternkrug. Little did they realize they had only postponed the inevitable by 25 years as the Russians would then arrive in Sternkrug. In 1945, several refugees were still around and they were told to leave everything and go. One started to say no because there was no place to go to and he was clubbed to death. This happened to all who did not go when told.

Mother was always ahead of my father. He just wanted to be left alone. Whatever had to be done on the house she had to push him – but he did it. She got trees from her mother and planted them in the garden. When they got married mother told me later she got 30 homespun linen sacks, good for holding 200 lbs. This was very important as this was farm thinking. She also got a loom chair. In later years I chopped it up for firewood. Industry had come to town and they made everything that farmers used to make on the loom. Mother took me to the city at times and there was lots to see for a little boy. She wondered why I fell so often, not realizing the city has many new things, which I saw and I did not watch my step.

All in all it was a good time for me. I ran barefoot all summer. Winters there was always lots of snow. It never failed to snow on Christmas Day. I usually got a Christmas tree out of the bush. Christmas Eve we usually had a play from school and when we arrived back home Santa Claus had been there, leaving lots of presents. We always had a dance 4 weeks before Christmas. Mother often told me about the time of the Kaiser.

She never spoke much of the war years. She used to go to market and taste the butter with a coin. There was always plenty in the market and cheap goods from the colonies. This was the time when Germany had colonies in Africa. Later the word colonialwaren changed to Lebensmittel. I always connected colonial with cheap wares which came free from the colonies. I never lost this thinking over the years.

Above: Manfred's parents, Martha-Ruth-Maria Pehike and Max-Karl-Otto Gutzke.

Roy: Much of what follows was told to me by my mother as she was more interested in events than my father.

I heard such names as Hindenburg – that name was always connected with something good. Then Bruning, which was said, `*Huat dem bruning auf die glatz das ihm die Notferordung platz'*. Apparently Bruning at one time had been chancellor and in the years of inflation and unemployment made an emergency decree. While he was bold headed and no-one liked him, she had the saying "hit him on the bold head that his emergency decree bursts" (this sounds better in the German language).

The inflation was in some ways not too bad for my parents as they had just started and had no money to lose. Mother said a million marks was good before noon, then the new rate to the dollar came out and a million would not buy a loaf of bread in the afternoon. Food was no problem to my parents as it was not plentiful but always enough as father always worked for the farmer and got food in return like bread, bacon, eggs, etc. The bread I really liked, we used to call it hasenbrot. I don't know where the name came from, but it means rabbit bread.

Sometimes I went with my father to the farms and had plenty to eat there. In the early 1930's mother used to go to the dentist frequently. She wanted gold on her front uppers. She managed to find the money for gold somewhere. I think it was 8 marks, then putting it in another 20 marks.

We had two dentists she considered in town, one was a dentist and one was a zahnartz (means tooth doctor, also dentist in English), both were Jewish. She liked it that way as she claimed Jews had better gold, a good reason not to go to the others. One day I had a tooth pulled – I didn't think much of it. I remember I had to rinse my mouth and the dentist had a blue glass to rinse with water. This really impressed me as I had drunk the blue water. This I told everybody. Next time I went to the dentist he explained to me that the glass was blue, not the water. I had never seen blue glass before and not many glasses other than wine and beer glasses. When we drank at home, and any other place, it was from a cup. Nobody would drink water from glasses.

Mother used to shop a lot for clothes and fabric. I hated this as it took her hours to decide and bargain as she never paid the listed price. She only went to the Jewish store. There were three clothes stores owned by Jews in the city – one richer than the others. Two names I remember are Jacobie Benjamin and Drucker Gunther. Then there was a third store where mother hardly ever shopped. He did not give her good bargains she claimed. She liked the one named Drucker. The other one was the rich one. In the 1930's he had an Opel Admiral convertible in front of his store, which was really something – a dream G.M. product, best of the line. I looked at that car quite often, whenever I was in town. It had real leather seats and it smelled good. This was the only one of these big cars in town.

Usually when I was in town with mother I got a half pound of candies. The real hard ones lasted for hours. We did not take the bus back which came through our village, despite it stopped right in front of our house, because the fare was 20 Pfennigs. Mother did not go on wagons at the local farmers because she claimed it was too hard for her to climb up so we had to walk the 4km.

In the early 1930's the Zigenner Gypsy's used to come through our village. It was said the Gypsy's stole children and we had to hide. We usually ran and hid behind the railroad embankment, 200 meters behind our house. We liked to see the Gypsy's when I was a little bigger – 8 to 9 years. I followed them as they had such nice painted wagons. The women had long hair and the men had earrings as they made meals in the wagon. It always smelled funny to us. When the Gypsy's stopped in town they had to park their wagons at the garbage dump. Then men with bears used to come around, the dancing bear type trained by men who made them perform for money.

One time I was close by and the bear got angry. I was so scared I could hardly run away. The bear growled real bad. He always had a mouth strap on so that they could not bite, but growl they certainly could.

Every so often der Billiger Kollex used to come around. This was a salesman with all his wares in front of him in a big leather container. Mother never bought anything from him. We kids sure liked him. *`Kollex Kollex Billage Ware'* was his slogan.

At times men dropped in at our door just asking for a piece of bread. Mother always gave them what they asked for as she did not like to see a hungry man. Some people knew how my mother was and took advantage of her. One woman in the village was a big lottery panhandler. All her money went to the lottery. When she had nothing to eat she was at our house free-loading. She promised mother part of the winnings when she won the grand pot. Well it never happened. Later, she moved away.

When I got to know the city and had learned how to ride a bike, which I learned two winters earlier, mother sent me to town for little odds and ends. One Sunday morning on the way to town I had to pass a few houses with some kids there who were always after everybody. I used to pedal like the devil to get by there. Not that I was ever beaten up, it was just that they threatened.

When I was about 5, I got drunk real bad by drinking all the left-overs in the glasses. I was not able to walk home I fell constantly.

The shoemaker had a daughter. She married a SA man in 1930. This SA man was killed in a motorcycle accident with my Uncle Albert in Kiefheider. I remember 6 SA men standing guard by his coffin and everybody in the village who did not want to offend the rising Nazis went and had a look at the spectacle the Nazis put on for one of their own. It was a good show. The daughter moved away afterwards. I never found out if the shoemaker ever was a Nazi or if he went to jail for two years for a stupid thing the Nazis found out about. After that he was just the village shoemaker. Sometime later he sold the house to a family with 7 children.

The new family was in the house for a few years at which point they had 11 or 12 children. Goering was Godfather to the 10th child. Later they wanted to settle in the east – the new German territories. It never came to that and in the end the Poles burned their house down in 1945.

Chapter Two: My View of the Rise of Nazi Germany

Roy - All this is good to read and heed. Times like that, I do NOT wish on anyone. Let's hope they never come again, anyplace. Be glad you did not have to go through such times. Before I can write you some more from the time during the war in Germany, I will have to write you some from the time before September 1939. Otherwise, things will not make sense to you.

After lots of turmoil in Germany in the 1920's and early 1930's, Hitler and his party was chosen to rule Germany as of January 30, 1933. He called it the third Reich and said it would last for 1000 years.

In the early 1930's there were all kinds of political parties in our village. It was the same all over Germany – communists, democrats, Stahlhelns, Nazis, Kaisertreve – just all parties. I liked to sit in the ditch along the street in front of the house when the shoemaker came back from the city on Saturday afternoon. He was always drunk and he had to make a left turn with his bike to his house. He never made it, he always ended up in the ditch where I, and others, were waiting for him. Also with us kids were some older folks. One of the elders was a good communist. As the shoemaker rode his bike into the ditch his wife would come out, join him and blame the communists for pushing him into the ditch. This was not true, but they blamed him anyway.

Every Saturday this resulted in an awful fight which lasted until sundown. Everybody was involved, even the wives. One Saturday I remember they raised the Wiesenbauna. This is a big wooden pole to hold the hay in place on the hay wagon. It takes a bit of strength to raise it. He did so and then wanted to drop it on the communist and crush him. It took a while before it came down. The commie sidestepped it and it managed to smash the neighbor's fence. The neighbor got into the fight and it kept up all week. Everything was quiet the following Saturday and then it started all over again.

This was about the time the National Sociastishe Deutshe Arbeiter party took over in Germany. The N.S.D.A.P or Nazis. I will say I remember that people were overjoyed, so elated, as it was not a real win at the ballot box. I had a funny feeling on the Brown shirts on what I had seen in years before. The same feeling was there again 10 years and 1 day later. More on this to come. The Nazis had made themselves felt in our region for some time. Whenever they had a meeting in town, they came in open trucks decked with fresh greenery from trees really festive. They defied the combined strength of the Communists, the Social Democrats and the rest of all the other splinter parties. They drove into town in open trucks. The leather belt on their cap under the chin meant we are ready for action. It was mostly the S.A. They always showed up in strength as they had recruited from the number of the unemployed, which were plentiful. They had different kinds of badges on their shirt collars which I liked to compare. Red, green, blue, white – all different colours. This was taken over from the army as the S.A. had secretly trained their men and the colour identified, just as in the army, red for artillery, white for infantry, in other words they had their own army. When the S.A. came by you always had to salute them, otherwise they would come out of the trucks and beat you up. The communists did not do that.

Once the Nazis were gone then came the communists, some on foot or on bikes, some in wagons, others in groups marching. They always had a band with them which played the Shallhasen, some kind of a horn instrument. They wore leather jackets, leather caps, and what I always thought were funny looking boots. When the communists came through the village I always had to go out and look. All this was especially big on May 1, 1932, the last May Day the other parties were on parade besides the Nazis or Brown shirts.

Some came back in the evening bandaged, which was a horror. One time at the end of 1932 the Nazis were run out of town. They were very low in standing and they took a licking. While all this was going on, elections were held. More people marched – you could have asked for a ride as the Nazis moved everything, especially if you promised to vote for them on election day. One day a big JU52 plane came overhead. It was not very high and I could see the open door. Out came leaflets by the thousands. I had several – one showed a farmer with his cattle being driven off by the brown shirts, so this must have given out by the communists. In any case there were not many planes. When one came over I used to run outside and look, and then this big JU52 dropping paper – really exciting. Little did I know that 11 years later I would again look at communist leaflets, in the same region.

One plane used to come at 4pm just about over our house we called it the mail plane. In all this turmoil of fighting, marching and elections, one day mother came and said Hindenburg had given Hitler the Kanzlership. This was on the 30 January 1933. On this date all the nonsense stopped. People realized something had happened without really knowing what it was. The men with the bears disappeared. Kollec went away no more gypsies. Nobody came begging for bread to our door anymore. Then gradually other things started, like the collection for the Nazis when every Sunday there was a collection for something different, like Winterhilfe Dentshe in Ausland. The Wintershilfe was quite good you could give 1 lbs. of food flour sugar etc. that was given to some poor folks or old ones with not much money. The winter of 1933 was the last time my father saw unemployment as a bricklayer and by the summer of 1934 he came home with 32 marks a week which was only part payment. Hours were 48 per week, 9 a day and Saturdays till noon. Pay for him at first was 1.20 mark per hour. He was guaranteed to get it as the party ruled. Bricklayers had to work for a master not on their own where they were cheated out of their pay. Like the time my father once built a barn he never saw the money for his labor. Then papers came around register for medical checkups do this, do that it was always something.

Although so slowly at first the Nazis eventually got their hold on everything. There was still one election to come in March 1933. This was really big. Placard flags and slogans everywhere. Papers showed you how to vote as there was only one party so now you only need Yes or No. A big yes a little No. It was said in our village that some people had been given pre-marked ballots as Nazis only ran the show by this time. The pre-marked ballets could never be proven on Monday when the papers printed the results. Our village was the worst in the group of people over 50 where they had “no” votes while all other were 98% Nazi. Our village had a poor house which was occupied by one woman and one family. Some suspected that this woman was one of the no voters. Well as long as the Nazis were there they never bothered her even though they had lots of reason to. Mother never liked the Nazis much. Then one day in 1934 she went through a drawer and she found the old Stempelbook from father. She realized he had not been out of work all winter, he had made good money – times were good. What happened next was mother called up and explained what she had found and thought things over and said she would make a big Nazi flag – the biggest in the village. She did this the very next day. As the 1st of May came we had the largest swastika of anyone in front of the house. Some cloth was left over from this so I got a little 2 square foot of cloth for a small swastika. Our neighbors always flew the black, white and red of the Kaiser. One day after the takeover a Nazi leader from the next village stopped at the neighbor and told them to take the flag down. He did so and never flew another one over all the years. We had all been expecting that he would be told to take down the Kaiser flag.

In March 1933, there were elections in Germany. Hitler's party had not gained a majority but it was the strongest over all the splinter parties. In 1933, he created the "Ermechtigungs Gesetz" (the full power law). March of 1933 was the last time that Germans would see free elections until 1946. Hitler's 1000 year Reich lasted 12 years, 3 months and 10 days. Some might say, and rightly so, that it was only 10 years and 3 days, since on the 2nd of February 1943, the German 6th Army surrendered at Stalingrad. This was in a way a victory for the Red Army, but the German "Wehrmacht" was still a formidable fighting force. The victory was to go to either the Nazis or Communists and the communists won. The battle of Kursk in Russia in 1943 saw the defeat of the Wehrmacht at the hands of the Red Army. After the battle of Kursk, the Red Army dictated where and when to fight in the east and the Wehrmacht never again started any offensive. The Wehrmacht fell back out of Russia and Poland to the river Elbe. That marked the end of a once proud army, beaten and defeated in the worst way. It was the first time in modern history that entire armed forces of a country surrendered and became prisoners of war. Up to 1939, a lot of the Polish army had escaped. Up to 1940, it was the same for France. However, up to 1945 no one escaped from the German armed forces.

By 1936, the thinking in Germany was like this: when the Nazi's came and took the communists away, I did not protest because I was not a communist. When they came and took the Jews away, I did not protest because I was not a Jew. When they took the Jehova's Witnesses away, I did not protest because I was not one of them either. When they came and took me away, there was no one left to protest.

In that time, it was best to walk quietly and say nothing. If you went to church on Sundays, the priest included Hitler in his blessings. If he did not do so, he would not be a priest much longer. it would be said that he would be transferred to another region, location unknown.

Hitler and his Nazi party had Germany in an uproar from the day he took office on January 30th, 1933. And all it took was about 2 years for the party to organize everything and everybody. You were free and you were human as long as you were for the party 100%. Everyone else, they soon found out. As soon as he took office in 1933, things settled down from the hectic years of the 1920s and early 1930s. By 1936 everything was well within party lines. You said "heil" when told, you went to marches when told. You did not dare stay away when a party speaker came to town to talk some glorious propaganda. You were watched invisibly all the time. Starting in 1936, new laws came out every so often, but they did not concern you or so you thought. If it did, it would have made no difference. There was no opposition. There was only one law. I did not understand much of this at the time. It had to do with sterilization. Anyone who was handicapped from birth got sterilized. About 1938 in our village, there were 2 couples who got involved with this. One couple had to wear glasses that were like the bottom of coke bottles. They had one child before the law came into effect. It just so happened that this child was okay. The other couple both were deaf. On top of that, they could only speak a few words. They were both about 50 and were deaf & dumb. They could do sign language and I remember them wearing a yellow armband with some dots which identified them as deaf. One day someone must have told them that they had to go to the hospital for the operation (there were no children). It is possible that the operation was not explained right to them. As it happened, some people did not return. This middle aged couple was just living by themselves and never bothered anybody. Both were partly on welfare. Whatever they thought of this operation, everyone was soon to find out. They waited on the railway line, threw themselves in front of the next train and both were killed. Such were the laws that the Nazi's created.

For the ordinary working man, things were just good as long as he held the party line and showed no opposition to anything. A worker had lots of work for a change and got paid every week. The law said so and no one would dare not pay a German worker every week. He got a vacation. He could travel with the help of his union. His family was well taken care of in the event that anything happened to him. A worker was king. If he had a big family, I think it was by the 8th child that father and mother got a document from the Reichsmarhall Herman Georing stating the he was the godfather to this child. By the time number 10 came around, he would get a letter from Adolf Hitler thanking them for such a big family. Adolf would be the godfather of child number 10 and up.

In case a worker had no radio in the 1930s, he could go to the Nazi party and say "I have no way of hearing any speeches of Hitler as I have no radio". The party office just asked the local burgermeister (mayor) about this man and within 3 weeks, this man had a Volks-Empaenger radio from the local party. Very simple and of no cost to him. The burgermeister always okayed the radio as he only had loyal citizens in his community. It was said the Volks-Empaenger and received the Deutschland Sender (German Station) with Goebbels talking but that was not so. It brought in foreign stations too.

Early in 1939, all of Germany was involved in a blackout exercise. This was supposed to last for one week. After 5 days, the Minister of Defense declared the blackout a success so it was terminated. It was good to see all of the lights on again as it was rather depressing in our city during the blackout. This was the first and last time that a minister of defense of the 3rd Reich would end a blackout. Next time the lights came back was different. It was ended when the Allied forces ended the last blackout. In a few months after this exercise, the lights in Germany would go out for real and when they came back on they were few and far between. Nobody had to tell people the years of horror and devastation were over as the few lights were a signal of a new beginning.

One day in August of 1939 a friend of my father came visiting us. He was from the next village. After a while of talking which centered on the coming war, this man asked my father if he knew when the next war would start. Of course, he did not know so this man wrote down a set of numbers of whatever Hitler had done. Then he asked my father to add the figures up. The result was 1.9.1939. History proved this man and his figures right.

As we were about 65 miles (100 km) from the Polish border, we could tell that something was going on in all the forest around us. A few days before Sept.1, 1939, you could go nowhere in the bush without tripping over soldiers. At this time, all of this backed up for 50 miles (80 km) from the border. When they started moving, it took 2 days to clear them out. Every morning when I went to work, I passed the barracks. One morning, I saw no soldiers in the square. I heard no commands echoing, it was just empty. During the day, we heard that the garrison of heavy artillery had moved out during the night. A few months later, the units returned in daylight with a big parade.

Roy: Now you have some of the background. It might help when you read the rest.

Chapter Three: School Years

School was in Roggow where I started at 6 years of age 1933. This was an eventful year in Germany and the events of 1933 ruled my life for the next 15 years. In later years I often heard my parents talk how hard life was before 1933 because there was not much money to buy food with, no work, inflation and political turmoil all the time. My father worked at times for the local farmers or in the bush during the winter.

The school I went to was a country school - grades one to four in one room, taught by one teacher for about 55 children. Grades 5 to 8, 4 grades in one room, also had only one teacher. I was the only one of 20 new enrollments who had a big bag of candies. I also was the only one in the class of the year that called itself 1926. I was born March 1927 so I was eligible for the 1926 class. I was able to keep up with the older ones because the age difference did not bother me. I was strong for my age. I had a fight with everyone in my class. I beat them all, even the older boys. In school I was one of the hardest fighters and I did not care who I was fighting. Every year I stole the apples from the teacher's garden. When I was in the lower grades my sister Charlotte was already in the upper classes. In the winter she was allowed to stay in Roggow with Grandmother after school. I had to walk 2KM home through the deep snow. I don't think I would have liked sleeping at grandmothers. I did go to her house to pick cherries which she had plenty of. Grandmother had only chickens in her old age. The beds were filled with straw and the stalls where they had kept pigs and cows joined right on to the house.

The first year in school was for only 2 hours a day 10 to 12 noon. Writing was on a slate plate with a slate pen (Griffel), the reverse for mathematics. The first letter we learned to write was I. In school we were about 40 children in one room. Grades 1-2-3 -4. The classroom had one electric light in the middle of the room. It was not much in the wintertime when it was still dark in the morning. By the time Grades 2-3-4 started hours were 7 to 12 in the summer time 8 to 1pm in the winter. The room had one coal fired stove. One way to school was 2 km. In the summer, we all walked barefoot. In the winter we had boots up to our ankles the snow was up to and over our knees. Having wet feet all day was usual. Nobody pitied us for it.

The books we had in the house were the Bible and a hymn song book, which is about as many books as most people had.

During the first year in school the teacher came into the class in the morning and said “good morning”. This was 1933. Some days we used to sing a religious song to begin. Then things gradually changed. Before I went to school there used to be lots of elections in Germany – 1931-1932 – every month or so. The election was always held in the schoolhouse where the ballot box was located. This ballot box was about 4 ½ ft. high and 2 feet square. It stood on the floor and looked like stained oak wood, quite nice. It had a lock but I don’t recall who held the key for it, very likely the Burgermiester.

I had only 2 hours instructions a day for the first few months in school. One day my sister came home and you would not believe what had happened. She was so excited. So was everyone. The

Above: Manfred and his two sisters in 1933. (Roy Gutzke Collection)

teacher had held an election with the upper classes in school. All made their own voting slip. As far as I know all asked for the Nazi party. There was a little boy in class, one of our neighbors, and he went into the ballot box and tallied up the slips one at a time. It was always yes. We smaller ones remembered this was the way to vote when we had an election. The teacher taught us how to make the ballot. She wrote two circles – yes and no – as by this time all other parties had been eliminated in Germany and you could only vote Nazis yes in a big circle or no in a circle you could hardly find. Then the teacher taught us how to read. He put the form on the blackboard and, in case you had forgotten, it was there for all to see. It was structured so that no one felt comfortable casting a no vote, which was a vote against the Nazis. The count in the end was all yes. It seemed no matter how we voted it was counted yes.

In May 1933 I came home one day and told my mother we have to greet the teacher from now on with HEIL HITLER in the morning. It used to be good morning Herr Lehrer. My mother did not like this at all, but the Nazi party came to rule Germany in January by dictatorship and that was the law.

The flag was in Germany Black – White – Red. No more; in 1933 the red swastika flag ruled. On big parades like the 1st of May you had to salute the flag or you got a lecture from Hitler's brown shirts. With age 10, I joined the Jungvolk, which means young folks, and was a precursor to the Hitler Youth, which was a must for all boys. I needed a uniform, but my parents did not buy it for me. I had to work as a cowboy in the summer to herd some farmer's cows to get paid 30 to 50 penning a day. This pay bought me a brown shirt but not much more. Two years later the war started and the clothes coupons couldn't buy a uniform. When we had enough money to buy the uniform we still couldn't buy one. Before the war there was a Jewish store which was bought out by some Nazi big shot, so they said the result was that while we could get our uniform from the Jew ironically we could not get from this Nazi big shot. The big Jewish traders that were still in Germany did not sell him anything. So much for kicking the Jews out.

In school I made every grade on time. We had an old teacher in the village who he had taught there for 32 years. His teaching was an absolute obedience and no nonsense approach. It was the only way you learned or he would wear his hazelwood stick out on you. I was glad when he retired in my 2nd year. After him we changed teachers quite often. We got more progressive ones, very much up to the times. The good ones did not last long as they got called to the city to work in the bigger schools. It was better for them, like a promotion. When I was in my 3rd year we had a new teacher fresh from teachers college - quite modern in his views. Not quite the full Nazi type, but already a little the Nazi way. In time we would get a full Nazi teacher. When I was in the 6th grade we got a new teacher again. Over 6 feet tall, sporty looking. He wore the Nazi badge on his lapel. It was said from the beginning he would not be with us very long. The war was on and he was of military age.

A new, very arrogant teacher arrived, and he spent much time screaming at the students. I did not like him. One day before he left he came into the classroom in a Black SS uniform. We had heard about the SS but did not know about them. Seeing him in the uniform shut-up every one. When the war was on he was one of the first ones to be called up. Our other teacher had to go to summer training camp during the vacation time every year. At times our regular teachers came back from the war, so did our regular ones during the campaign in France, 1940. Things were going well in France and teachers were needed at home. I remember France capitulated. We went out, hoisted the Nazi flag, sang patriotic songs – and we had 2 hours off. This was a great day.

By the third year this teacher was an NCO and he got called up. We had no school for quite some time, then a lady teacher came for a while. The school closing, came and went throughout the war. We didn't learn much after 1941. For myself the time missed was regrettable. I liked to learn and once I understood all the problems, learning came easily to me. Once the Nazi teacher asked me if I wanted to go to teachers college. This would have been good for me. It meant, of course, going away from home. I asked my parents what they thought about it as it meant leaving home. The idea was brushed aside right away. People did not leave the village unless they absolutely had to and this was not considered a good reason. In less than two years I left home anyway.

As a boy up to the age of 15, I never went further away than 10 KM from the place where I was born. That was the way it was at that time. Where would you want to go anyway? My father suffered from Asthma which he claimed he got from a gas attack in France in the First World War. Sometimes he smoked one Cigar a day. The Cigar was 10 pennies that was all he could afford and very seldom he bought a bottle of beer. My father was well known in the village and very often he was asked to come and do some building work for all kinds of people. Later on he was even the commander of the volunteer fire department. Where he came from is unknown, but he had a sister and a brother. The sister, Anna, was in Roggow with my Grandmother and his brother had a house there and 2 acres land in a village 9km from us. We had good contact with both. His sister had 2 children, his brother 5. By 1930 there were 14 of us with the name Gutzke. I remember some years he went on "Stempeln" (unemployment insurance) at 8 marks a week. Mother told me at times she heard people say in the lineup for welfare they had to eat Kernssee fat and grease. Well, 8 marks was not much. Mother added some money by sewing ladies dresses and wedding dresses. My mother did some sewing to supplement the income, for which she got 2 to 3 marks for a dress and 4 marks for a wedding dress.

Most of the time I had to deliver the dresses. Mother said charge 3.25 mark. I used to ask them for 3.50 mark. 25 cents for me, but only where I knew folks had money and paid me on delivery. Still I got some delivery money anyway. I did not like delivering dresses.

It was a good time at home before school whenever mother had a wedding invitation because I would go along with her. Martha and her shadow as people used to say. Mother always made arrangements so that she didn't play in the band on wedding days. She had to pay the band for doing it and money we had none. One thing I know I liked the weddings. Lots of good food. We also had an uncle in Krifheide working for the railway. We visited him at times. They had 5 children one was run over by a train when he was about 12 years old.

In Pomerania, Germany, which is now Poland, we had very cold winters with lots of snow. About the end of March my hands and heels started to itch for days. After a few days some boils came up on my fingers and the frostbite came out the skin broke up it was a mess for a few days. I had bandages on my hands and heels. One year it must have been about 1938 the doctor put something on my fingers and since then they never broke out again. I still have the scars .

The house had 3 rooms. The kitchen was on the main floor and upstairs were two rooms. In the winter the living room was heated. The bedrooms were cold. We would put a brick in the oven, heat it up at bedtime, wrap it in a cloth and then you took it to bed with you to keep your feet warm.

Sometimes we had an earthenware water bottle with hot water at our feet. Other times the blankets were warmed up in the oven. Before going to bed, as children, we looked under the bed to make sure nobody was under there. Who or what this was supposed to be we never found out. From school we were given homework in the winter. If you didn't do it right after school at home you were out of luck because it got dark around 4pm. My mother had the petroleum lamp only for her sewing otherwise you sat in the dark. Electricity came to the village in 1938. Standards at that time was a single 15 amp fuse per house, unthinkable by today's standards.

Chapter Four: Life Under the Nazis

Roy: All the rest is from my own memory.

In 1934, my second year in school, we went on a day outing with the class. The class went out under the swastika flag, which I carried in front. We went 6 km to a village where they had a big clay pit and made brick. We were told the factory had suffered in the last years and work and production was not at full blast. We could see lots of workers and the whole place looked very clean. We were shown where the worker's lunch room was located. It was run and managed under the Nazi organization K.D.F. Kraft – Strength through joy - or the one and only union – all other workers unions had disappeared or were forbidden. This lunchroom contained nice tables and chairs and a place to keep the coffee warm, a paper stand and a woman who looked after things. It also had Hitler's picture on one end of the hall. We were told all this had been built in the last years as before the workers had to eat outside wherever they were, if they had a job at all. Now they had a good lunchroom and a place for bikes, good pay and lots of work. The party was proud of what they had accomplished at this place. It was a good improvement.

People did not know what to make of all the Nazi propaganda that came their way. It was all new to them to belong to something. One morning mother came to me and said the Reichstag had burned down. I could tell she was angry and sorry as Hindenburg represented the Reichstag. Later on Von Der Lubbe, a Dutch communist, was blamed for it. This, as far as I remember, cooled people off. It made one thing suddenly clear, how organized the police had become in a few months, to follow this up so quickly.

We had some relatives in a city 30 km from us to the north, Koshin, at times we visited there. One day we were there and heard Hindenburg had died. In Koshin there was a big parade and a 21 gun salute for his funeral. From this day on I always thought Hindenburg had been buried in Koshin as it must have made quite an impression on me, a 7 year old. After Hindenburg's death the currency changed quite often. I liked the new look of it.

This family also had a movie projector. I watched some movies which I did not understand, and made no sense to me as it just flashed on the screen. From the two boys I got a homemade biplane as a present and surely liked it and played many hours with it in the garden. Mother started to tell me why I could not make such a plane. How could I? I had never seen a plane on the ground. Overall 1933 through 1935 were not bad years. All that time we heard about the big German Luftschiffe (airships). The Hindenburg and the Graf Zeppelin always had their locations reported in the paper every day. I followed the flights around the world. Surely, I thought they would love to come around our area as it was near the flight path. On this trip they did not come. Then one day I read in the paper the Hindenburg and the Zeppelin were on a trip all over Germany.

This took quite a long time. After a few days Mother said "better look out tomorrow, the Zeppelin is coming."

To this day I remember looking for them. As I knew where they would show up I watched a long time and nothing came. I started to play in the garden. All of a sudden something made me look up and there was the Hindenburg – awful big – just hanging there. I thought it was 300 meters away from me – so big and silver. At first I could do nothing, then I ran to the window where my mother was sewing dresses. I knocked on the glass. How I didn't shatter it in the excitement I don't know. I could hardly speak.

After that I turned back and there were two warships and the Graf Zeppelin not far behind, slimmer and not quite as gigantic. I started running along the street as I wanted them to be directly over me. While running along the street I made such a racket everybody knew at once what was going on. After some distance I realized they were just plain big and the distance they were was 14km by road, 4 to 5 km by air. They were not very high, just hanging there and cruising along. Some people said they heard music coming from the ships.

What a sight – the big Hindenburg up front, the Graf Zeppelin not far behind. My long-time dream of seeing them had finally come true. Later reports put the ships 25 minutes behind schedule and 1 ½ km. off course to the north as they had to fight westerly winds.

During these years my father was always busy. He had established himself as a good bricklayer and one architect always called on him when he had some hard intricate brick work like arches, circles and corners. In 1936 the garrison of the local army artillery was expanded. Two more barracks were added to the existing one. He worked on this as it was only 3 km from home. It took all year and it was a big complex, 12 large buildings. This was called the Hindersin Kaserne after some general. He did not realize while working here that he would be a soldier himself in three years and get called to duty in the barracks he helped build.

All the time father made good money, so one day he said I should have a bike because I was using my sisters and forever wrecking it. Next Saturday he said he would buy one, which cost 54 marks and was expensive because bikes were in short supply in Germany. The money was there but no bike because all the steel went to armaments so no bikes. Three weeks later I got one.

Above: Charlotte's confirmation day. 1936.

At times the circus came to town. Big Circus Krone. They plastered every tree and barn door with their colourful papers. I had bad luck and had a big boil on one of my eyes and wore an eye patch. We had some friends not too far from the circus. We left the bikes there.

In 1936 the Olympics were in Berlin and everyone followed events closely. Every day the medals got counted and everything was discussed at length. As I had to walk 2 km to school, we had a few flags in a group. We walked together and talked all the way to school. There was a battle with the Stalinists and Ethiopians for a time. We always discussed that. Too bad the Italians won in the end as we didn't like that result.

One time when I was with my grandmother, she showed me a mother cross which had been issued by the Nazi party for women who had 4 or more children. Later I thought this over and came up with only 3 of her children. That was Fritz or Olle, Tante (Aunt) Anna, and my mother. After a few days I asked my mother about the 4th child. I mentioned grandmother had shown me her cross. I got a very evasive answer. I did not pursue this any further. The answer must have been satisfactory.

As I mentioned before, our village had a poor house. One woman lived there. She had a boy with her about my age. The man had died quite young. This woman never worked. She just walked around and talked a lot. She was a living newspaper. She also came to our house at times. I did not like her at all. She was just a loudmouth. I was told to be nice to her son. He was alright at that age, just a playmate. One time he set fire to a farmers baking house and wood. For this, he was locked up for 10 years, as the farmer happened to be a big party member. The loss in the fire was about 100 marks. Later on in the war, all inmates with trouble like this were asked to join the army. The sentence was then commuted. The reason I write this is as follows. In about 1936, all school children had to make a family tree. It was good to go back as far as possible. My ancestors were traced to 1812 by my sister. Not the boy from the woman in the poor house had only his mother and father. Naturally his mother knew her mother but she never said who it was. Then she did not know who her father was. She pressed her mother for it. It was useless, it never came out. Nobody except this woman knew who the father to the woman in the poor house was. Forty years later (from 1935 to 1975), I heard who the woman in the poorhouse was. It was the 4th child of my grandmother. A well-kept secret.

In 1937 the barracks that father had helped to build got new recruits. Motorized 10.5 artillery used to come with their half-tracks along our street. At first we thought it was some kind of monster. The soldiers trained in the nearby fields and the bush almost every day. Whenever I was out of school I used to watch them. School had changed gradually. Religious songs in the morning were the first thing removed – no more songs. Our old teacher had retired and got a big send off with torchlight parade and all sorts of other gifts.

The boys 10 and older had joined the Hitler youth as there were no more Pathfinders or Boy Scouts. There was one good thing though. At first all members of the Hitler youth had no more school on Saturdays. Around 10am they could go on this, their duty marching and sport. Not all boys were in the Hitler Youth at first. Membership cost 10 cents a month and it was 4 hours duty a week; 2 hours every Wednesday evenings and 2 hours every Saturday. I always envied the bigger boys when they went out of school on Saturday. By the time I was 10 in 1937 everybody had to be in the Hitler youth. Saturday off was no more. It was more Saturday afternoon or Sunday morning. With all this Hiel Hitler we had to quote short sentences by Hitler or Goering in the morning in school. Every day one other child had the same quote and it was hard to find some new ones after a while. All you had to say was Hitler said there *`die arbeit achte den arbeiter'*. Honor the work. Honor the worker. Just things like that. Then one hour religions instructions a week, which fell flat most of the time. Nobody ever wanted you to know who Moses was. As long as you knew all the ministers of the N.S.D.A.P you were all right and passed grade.

Every so often a speaker used to visit. This was always at 8pm in the local dance hall. In school we had to learn a song for it as an opening to the speech. What made no sense to us is that we had to stand for the entire speech so we could sing the Horst Wessel song. I can truly say I never liked this. I hated it.

My joining at the age of 10 started on a sour note. All boys in my class joined at the age of 10. I knew they needed some kind of a leader so I watched the older ones and then I was chosen for the 10 year olds. One evening I set duty and the boys came to raise hell so no duty next day. I was nobody but I could wait my time. Which I did and in the end I beat them all out. But more on that later.

One summer, mother had a lady visitor that I had never seen before at home. She was from a neighboring village. What made it so interesting was she had been in America. She had just come back to get her 2 boys about age 12 to 14. Emigration from Germany was not encouraged at the time of the 3rd Reich, especially not for the boys. It just so happened the boy had bad eyesight, which was a loss to the state so they could go. It was not long and the lady was back once more at our house and then they left.

While at our place, I heard her talk about New York. I had never heard anything like it. She really made the skyscrapers seem big and there were several of them. I questioned mother on this several times. I was told America was the land of the unlimited possibilities, skyscrapers which really scratched the clouds. From then on I often looked towards the west on clear days as if I could see the skyscrapers. Others said America was the land of milk and honey. I knew Zeppelins flew there often and Max Scheming was always boxing in New York. One time I heard about Chicago and Al Capone, but in general not much was heard from America. The land has had a spell on me ever since that time.

We also had some bible thumpers in the village, a sect which did not bother anybody, but religion was not much liked by the 3rd Reich. One morning I got up and mother told me they had taken the bible thumpers away. The ones in the other village were warned to burn their books. They did not do so. They too ended up in a concentration camp. One was the village blacksmith. All the farmers then went to the party as they had no one to shoe their horses. Within a week he was back. He had to sign that he did not want to bother with politics. He did not and was now free to do his work. The lady in our village came back in 2 years after she signed too. Nobody ever heard where she had been. Later in the war she became a train conductor and was run over and lost a leg. She was rehabilitated.

In the meantime the soldiers in the barracks had basic training. I used to watch the changing of the guard at 12 noon. Soldiers were on leave in the village and one got friendly with a girl from the local farmer. It was nearly to the point of marriage. One time the soldier was at our house as Emil Johns was the girl's uncle. Then one morning father had left for work and he was back in no time. He said come and have a look. I jumped on the bike and had a look at him hanging there. The soldier hung himself at Johns' stall, which could not be seen from the street.

This was the farmer where we used to buy our milk. Well, I just did not go back there, afraid of what the hanging one would do me. Something I always liked was hot chocolate. On Sunday morning I could only have it if I got the milk myself. I walked very carefully so that I would not fall and spill the milk on my way back 50 yards from home, but on the plain street I fell. The hanging one had pushed me. That really did it for me. I did not go back for several years.

After the Army Barracks were finished in the city, my father worked on a large hospital which was built to support the big Garrison the city now had. This was about the last large contract with a magazine for stores. Work was always full blast, 48 and more hours per week. Now the Nazi unions were well established. Workers even got vacation one week a year, then 2 weeks. This was never heard of before. One day the paper carried big ads. Go to Kolberg a city some 40KM north of us on the Baltic Sea. The fare was one mark per person return. This was hard to believe. The first train could hodd 1000 people but did not sell so good, but the next Sunday you had to have your tickets by Thursday. People had heard it was true. One mark and all had a good time. We went about twice a year.

At about this time mother had discovered movies at the matinee on Sunday afternoon. She took the 30 pfennig seat, the first two rows, she claimed no-one blocked her view there. She liked the ones with Laurel and Hardy. Shortly after this time movies became very popular.

Some people had battery powered radios – big things with the radio and the speaker separate. I could never figure out how the man got in that box. We used to listen by the local farmer in the village. Whenever Hitler spoke he always claimed the battery was flat, so I never heard that voice until we had our own radio in 1939.

One day an engineer* happened to drive through the village and he noticed no electricity, even though the line was 1 km off. That same summer we had electric light. Before that everything was petroleum light. After people had power in the house everything was better again. Heaters, stoves and all kinds of other things came in. It was a good time.

At times we had free movies from the K.D.F. organization at the local inn and they showed free patriotic films which dealt with Germany the good or the fatherland. They were well received. The party had made a lot of believers after Hitler went into the Rhineland – even the holdouts got a Swastika flag in 1936.

Lots of times I went into the bush to collect mushrooms. A man in a truck would come twice a week to pick them up and he always paid cash right away with nice shiny coins. For one pound I got about 15 pfennig, not much but it was good money and it bought a lot at that time. My allowance was about 10 pfennig a week – that was enough for candies.

One day we came back from school in 1937 and I saw a strange structure on top of a distant hill. This day after day went higher

* we think that Manfred meant engineer. ED

and higher. On completion, it was a tower. In the meantime, towers had sprung up all over the country on hilltops. Some had 6 corners, higher ones had 8. One day I visited one. As it was said, on the top of the platform was a box with a turret which in case of war could shoot the planes down. This was not so. They were for survey purposes. The one I was on was high for me as I did not like heights. Anyway, on clear days from this tower, you could see the Baltic Sea, a 40 km distance. Another hill was used by the Hitler Jugend for gliders. It faced in the wind, the trees were cut and the glider pulled by a large rubber slingshot. I watched this quite often as it was just a short distance from home. If you had in mind joining the Luftwaffe air force, later on you could join the flieger Hitler Jugend (Hitler Youth Fliers). Here you learned to fly a glider. On a windy day, this place was very busy.

As most of the work was done in town, father heard one day that he was to go about 140 km to work on a project for 6 weeks. Others had been there before him and they liked the work but six weeks was all you could get. Pay was higher and you had cheaper rail fare while there. When he came back he said they were building big round things in the ground – sometimes half a round – and when it was nearly finished the army came and took over. He said he had been in Peenemunde, an island on the Baltic not far from us. This had no meaning to us, it was just Peenemunde.

In 1938 we had 2 acres of land and two meters from the house the land was planted with potatoes. At harvest time mother picked all the potatoes by herself and I, with the bike, put a little wagon on the back and for 2 ½ days I pulled potatoes. I got everyone home. On the second day, around noon, on a really nice fall day, mother said to me "look up in the sky and tell me what you see".

What I saw, heaven behold, was absolutely unbelievable. I saw two suns in the sky! Mother said she saw them too. This was in 1938 and I have never seen anything like it since.

Our area had good soil for potatoes. Every farmer lad lots of acreage under the plough with potatoes. The harvest was always important. In 3 to 4 weeks, everything had to be out. In 1938 while mother was at the farmers digging potatoes, I herded his cows for 11 days from sun-up to sun-down, a simple rule. A good farmer paid 50 pfennigs per day plus food and I was with a farmer who paid me 50 pfennigs. At the end, father came to take me home. He asked what I wanted. The money, or should he buy me something? I opted for the money as I had been in the Hitler Jugend for a year and I needed a brown shirt. From this money, 5 marks and 50 pfennigs mother bought me a brown shirt. Father asked the farmer what he had in mind to buy. He said he would have bought me an air rifle. In the end, the potato harvest was hard work as there was some frost on the ground in the morning. This year, 1938, was the only year I herded cows for any length of time. I had done so at times for a day or two. In 1939, I had made my mind up that I wanted some money, digging potatoes paid 3 to 3.50 marks a day. I had heard how hard it was crouching on your knees all day and the 3rd to 4th day, it would be really bad. It was like that. But I lasted 20 days and had lots of money. Next year, I emptied baskets for the diggers. That was harder work, in a way, you had to walk over a plowed field all day. I listened a lot to the ongoing talk as everybody had stories from the past 11 months. One lady in the crowd had read the 6th to the 10th book of Moses.

She talked about this on and off. I had to go home after that through the bush. One year we had roggen (rye) on the field where we had potatoes other years. This happened to just be the years where all the men were away at the army. The roggen (rye) had to be cut. Mother worried for a long time how she would get to it. It just so happened father had taught me how to cut grass with a scythe before he left. I figured I could manage and cut the roggen (rye) even though the scythe had to have an attachment and was heavy for a 13 year old. I started one morning and did not let up till I had it done. Later I heard from some experienced men that this had been a big feat for a 13 year old. After that, I could do anything.

This year of 1938 was just plain awful. Hitler always had a crisis going. Father worked at a sawmill on a house and when there was one of Hitler's emergencies we phoned over the rail phone to him as the postman had delivered a telegram. This meant report at once to the next army post. Over the year there had been physicals on men and every one of them was classified. Father, for that time, was classified as Ersatz Reserve 1. Replacement reserve – in other words first to be called to active duty. This is how it happened that he got to be a soldier in the barracks he helped build a few years earlier. He was away for a few weeks at a time but things were never the same after the fall of 1938.

Father had been a prisoner in Russia in the First World War and later in Flanders Field. I often asked him who he considered the best fighters after the Germans as I was reading in his army book years later. He was very likely in action against the Canadians. He never spoke much about the western front, hated the English, artillery for days on end and barbwire. Outside of that I heard nothing. One time I had a bad sunburn and was in bed a few days. In the evening he came and told me some stories from the war – all about Russia. How he was shot at by Russian snipers from treetops. This did not last long as they had a machine gun company nearby and they were called in and shot up the bush for half a day.

In school in 1938 we had lots of politics. I remember the teacher making it quite clear that we understood Germany was a dictatorship. He claimed this was good – we had never seen anything different so it was good to us, so how could we compare? All other nations had the depression and nationalism was good to us.

One evening a plane started cruising our area. The army had training searchlights that went on and tried to find the plane. They did this at times quite fast. Other times the army had training which was called a bivouac where they slept in the field. This was really exciting for me. The units simulated a battlefield and all kinds of different flares were fired practically all the time. This was an omen of things to come. At times behind our house on the railway towards the Polish border, there were trains lined up from the army for miles. At times they had one extra locomotive to push the train. On the street, soldiers were marching at night, 3 days marching to Poland in the daytime. They were in the bush so nothing was to be seen. In 1939 the time of war was quite clear – most people were picking for the harvest. As I was in farming country nobody dared to ruin the harvest as that was always the most important thing to everybody there.

At times our village had soldiers quartered in private homes. One time our teacher had the bright idea to bring in an army instructor with a machine gun. He explained everything in class and the boys were very interested. It impressed me that the gun could fire up to 500 rounds per minute. It was water cooled and could be made to be pulled like a sled in snow. By the time I was in the army, this gun was out of use and a real killer machine had taken its place.

Around our village were lots of forests and the soldiers from the nearby town Belgard came here to train quite often. Whenever I was at home and saw the soldiers marching in the bush, I followed them. It was always very interesting as lots of times the soldiers used blank ammunition. Also, as the Wehrmacht got built up under the 3rd Reich with Hitler, the soldiers had new and different weapons like new anti-tank guns and new motor vehicles.

While I watched the German Wehrmacht train here, I had no idea nor had anyone else, that this training in less than 7 years from now in 1945, this would be needed for real. The Wehrmacht would have a real opponent in the forest and not blue and red bands around the helmets. The real enemy was the Soviet army including Polish units who regrouped and got ready for their last assault which would carry them to the Baltic Sea at Kolberg-Koslin. While this was for real, the Wehrmacht did not win anymore. No boys with them anymore to watch them in action. Most people had left when they heard the Red Army was coming closer. While our village was located on a good highway, the Soviet tanks just roared through. In Belgard, the siren was blaring for the last time. Not for an air raid, the Soviet army was coming to take the city in early March 1945.

Twice a week, there was a big ritual at our house. Father shaved Wednesday and Sunday mornings. It was always a big setup. The knife sharpened on a leather strap. Then lathered up with a stick of soap and the shaving was something else. In 1938, father finally got a blade razor for his birthday. The first time with a blade, we all watched and to our surprise, it shaved with no cuts.

One visit I remember in 1939 my cousin Kurt had come back from Spain with the Condor legion. He was with the 88 anti-aircraft guns and he used to talk to others about the gun. I heard all this and decided in 1939 to join the 88 flak. Little did I know that within 5 years I was an 88 flak Kanamier loader. My other uncle Fritz, brother to mother, had been with admiral Sheers Matrosen in the 1st World War. He was in the battle of Jutland and later he was in the Hilfskreutzer (the Red Cross) Greif which tried to be a blockade breaker. They tried to break out of the North Sea via Shetland in 1917. He was sunk by English warships in the North Sea 1917. He was rescued after 4 hours in the water. By the time he was pulled out he was spitting blood. On board the English ship he was locked up with others in the pigs stall. The English told him we were already waiting for you. They knew that the Greif had left harbor. He returned to Germany in 1920. He worked on the railroad and took an early retirement with pension in late 1920. I have never seen him doing a day's work in his lifetime. On the 1st of the month he got his pension which was very good. He went through to the next bar and got drunk but he had enough sense before he got drunk that he always bought a liter 98 per cent spirits. After he was drunk he came to our house and father took the ½ of his bottle and made schnapps from his spirits. Then he put water in Uncle's bottle and it was full again. Uncle Fritz spoke some English and he taught my mother some. With that she always told me she had to write to prisoner of war. I learned to count to 10 from mother in English. Little did she realize in a few years she had to write the same words again to a POW. This time to her son when I was a prisoner in England.

So father always had enough to drink for the month. We kids made fun of him because he always wanted to know if we knew Admiral Sheers Matrosen. I used to say yes. He was very proud of it and I got one dime. I did this several times and it meant a dime every time. He also wanted to know if I would join the Navy. I never told him I would so I got no dime for that. The son of our tenant upstairs said he would and he got a dime for that. This boy was true to his word and within 3 years he would be with the submarines.

When Uncle Fritz was not drunk he could do a good days work as he was as strong as a bull of good health. I liked to ride his bike of which he had the very best. When he was hit by a car he was on the bike and it was quite badly smashed. It was put in for repair the cost was 8 mark and I had that much in the bank. I took that out, closed the account and paid for the repair so that I could have the bike. I was not asked too much by my mother how I had got hold of the bike. One year Fritz or Olle helped us butcher a pig in December. In the afternoon he was quite drunk and mother did not know how he could be drunk as she said we had nothing to drink in the house. She had forgotten she made 25 liters of wine in the fall from cherries and it was sitting in the den for settling and aging. Olle had found the siphoning hose. He put that in the big bottle and had a good drink every so often. This was his last time he helped butcher a pig. Olle had the Iron Cross 2nd Class and other medals which my mother said were placed in his coffin. I later wore his Navy uniform to school.

Uncle Fritz never liked the son of his sister Anna. When he heard that Gerhard would get married in 1940, he swore months in advance that he would not go to the wedding. Even so, it meant losing free drinks and it did not cost him anything to travel there because he had a free railroad pass. With this,

Uncle Fritz as we called him, was true to his oath. He never did go to the wedding. The evening of the wedding, he was run over by a car and was killed. The car belonged to a doctor in town. My uncle as usual was drunk like a sailor. Mother tried to sue the doctor. It was useless. On the morning my sister and I got ready to go to the train very early in the morning Mother said to me Uncle Fritz is dead. All I could say or think of at the moment was what will grandmother say, will she be happy now? Grandmother had quite a cross to bear over the years seeing him drunk so often. My mother said that she didn't forget he was her son. I remember that to this day - a mother forgets and forgives. My grandmother was about 75 years old when I got to understand who she was in the family. In 1930, she lived in a house that was about 150 years old. Straw on the roof the entrance a big stone as a step then a den and the door to the smokehouse. Then a large room and another big room and kitchen. The smoke from the kitchen fire served for the smokehouse.

The smokehouse was about 10 foot square on the bottom then it tapered off and it became the chimney. This was the only iron in the house, the rest was clay. When standing on the floor of the smokehouse you could see right up to the sky. Grandmother never used glasses and at 80 years she used to read the local paper. When I visited her she was always behind the spinning wheel, spinning sheep's wool mostly for the local farmers. Most of the time it was for farmer Haas. He was the one which had given mother the lumber for the house. She charged 3 marks for what was called a large. On a good day with clean wool she did one large. Then she watched who had died in the village. She told me she used to watch if someone had died in between Christmas and New Year's. If so then she knew 12 more would die during the year in the village. This superstition had something to do with the 12 holy nights around Christmas. I never understood this superstition but her predictions were absolutely true. She knew such things.

One year I was about 10 or 11. I had a wart in my hand. It bothered me quite a bit. Medication was not so good at this time. I used to cut it off but it grew back every time. Then near the middle of the year my mother told me how to get rid of the wart once and for all. The story she told me she heard from her mother when she was a little girl. I had to wait for the 15 of June in between 11 and 12 o'clock. The 15th of June is the middle of the year middle of the month 11 to 12 o'clock middle of the day. So 3 times the middle. Nobody will believe this nowadays. I should take a knife to school and make the wart bleed. While doing this I had to say 3 times I believe in God the father and the holy ghost amen. I was not to say anything about this as long as the wart was in the stages of disappearing and I had to believe in it. I kept this word and did not say anything as long as the wart was still there. Needless to say the wart went away with this hocus pocus and I have not had another one to this day.

Whenever I had a cut on my foot or hand, I used to go out to our field a distance and put the black earth on the wound. It always stopped bleeding and healed. At times I also used some broad leaf plants, which worked as well.

One year I broke my thumb falling with the bike. I was hit by a boy with another bike. The bone just about came out. The hand got real thick and it hurt like hell all the time. In the morning my mother said get up and go to Belgard. There Tante (Aunt) Geide she will take you to the local wood shoe maker and he will blow on it. So I went there The Tante took me to the Shoemaker he did his blowing Hocus Pocus it stopped hurting at once. He was no medical man. Otherwise he would have said it is a break go see the doctor. But he could take the pain away. Three days later the hand was still swollen. Mother sent me to Doctor Giede. I had to go to the Hospital for 3 days. He could not understand why I had not come before as the pain must have been terrible. I could not tell him what had taken the pain away. Some 35 years later I told Doctor Giede about this and he figured out that I had seen the wood shoe maker that time.

Our tenants were Emil Jahn, his wife and 2 boys. My parents were the only folks in the village who had the same tenant all the time. Rent was 12 Marks per month. Mrs. Jahn was from the next village 4 KM to the east of us. Her grandmother used to come over once a year for a visit in the winter time. It got dark early we had no electric light the first years. We sat in the dark and the old lady about 70 in the 1930's used to tell us some really terrific horror stories, absolutely gruesome. She could hear at night sounds like the ghosts and she said she used to walk in the middle of the road so that the hounds of the ghost would not bite her. She said when the animals on the farm were sick, the farmer plugged all the cracks in the stall so the animals suffocated. At the end of all the stories was always a cross and that took care of all the ghosts. In one story, an old poor man came out of the bush carrying a bundle of wood. He was very sad. His wife was sick and his children had nothing to eat. To add to all his misery the ghost caught up with him and the man was really scared. He was told not to be scared by the ghost. He found the old man of good heart and nature. After telling the ghost all his troubles. He was told to go home. He picked up his bundle of wood and went on his way. After a while the wood got very heavy. He barely made it home. He knocked on the door exhausted and he found the bundle of wood had turned to gold by the ghost.

Another story was that a man had a contract to build a church by a certain date. As the day came nearer, the man realized he would not finish in time. In his anger he called on the devil all of a sudden. A man appeared out of nowhere and the man offered to help him. All the contractor had to do was sign a new contract which the man gave him. The only catch was the contractor had to sign with his own blood. This he did. When the contract was signed the stranger promised to finish the church on the given date before the first rooster crowed. As the stranger left the man happened to see his footprints. It was one human print and one cloven print like a horse. The builder knew at once he had made a pact with the devil and he had signed his life away with his own blood. All the time the builder watched the progress of the church and he realized he would lose. Then he had a great idea. On the morning the church was to be finished and the devil had a few more stones to lay, he emitted the crowing of a rooster. A real rooster nearby heard this and started to crow just as the devil was on his last stone. Hearing the rooster, the devil went off picked up a big boulder and dropped it on the church. He smashed everything except a little part of the wall. She said that this story is true and that if we wanted to see it we could go to Grop Tyelow a village 14 KM to the south of ours. Years later when I was in the Hitler Youth I was camped on an outing in this village. I remembered this story from her and honestly have beheld there was this big boulder dropped by the devil surrounded by part of a wall in the center of the cemetery. The graves inscriptions were several hundred years old. The boulder is about the size of half a bungalow of today's standard size buildings.

Her stories were so frightening at times that my sister and I did not dare to go downstairs in the dark in the same house. The stories were very likely passed on to her by her mother so when I listened to them they were at least over 120 years old. The area in Pomumania is quite swampy with moors, lakes and the way she talked there was a sunken Kings Carriage in every swamp. There was always a light in the swamp and it made the carriage man drive towards the light at night. Then he just disappeared in the swamp. I have seen those lights. They are like a glow from rotten wood a true - a phosphorescent glow that with the darkness in the bush and the stories that were told, anyone would be scared to travel through the bush at night. If you knew the way very well you were not fooled by the lights. This grandmother passed away in the mid 1930's.

At Easter time we used to go and get Easter water. This had to be done before sunrise from a river flowing East to West and you should not speak a word on your way to and from. Once you spoke one word the spell of the water was gone. You washed in it and it was supposedly to give you good and nice skin all year. Another custom was Stiepen. This was done on Easter morning with new birch twigs on anyone you found in bed. You said with it, "Stiep Stiep Osteret Gibst Du Mir Kein Osteret Stiep Ich Dir Das Hemd Entzwet". (Stiep Steip Easter egg give me an egg or I step till it tears your shirt.) To get hit on your rear with these birch twigs really hurt. It was a good old custom.

The house my parents lived in had a kitchen and 3 rooms downstairs and a kitchen with 2 rooms upstairs, which was rented. There was also a stall for 2 goats, 2 pigs, chickens and ducks next to the stall. There was also a laundry room with an oven and a smokehouse. This was all built 1927. I remember helping my father in later years to finish the laundry room. We had an outhouse and an outside well 7 to 8 meters deep. One of my cousins used to say this was the best fresh water on earth. This cousin was the daughter of my father's sister, who had 2 children. Hertha and Alwin born about 1910-12. Hertha married the local schoolteacher in 1930. Alwin went to learn business in a grocery store, named Kolonialalwaren, after school. Note the name Kolonial. After a few years he joined the army in the early 1930's. He was stationed in East Prussia. When the army expanded in the 1930's he became an Underofficer then a Feldwebel. His Mother was very proud of him as her husband had been an Underofficer in the Kaisers army he had given his life in the field of glory in 1916. I remember quite a big picture in the honour of Underofficer Kath. It showed a soldier on the ground with his head on his pack an angel with an olive branch over the dead hero. Soon her son became Oberfeldwebel. She went along the village street telling everybody Alwin made Oberfeldwebel. That was higher than anyone ever made it in the village except one that made Lieutenant who was from the family mother had got the lumber from to finish the house. The Lieutenant fell in the field of glory too. This loss was really felt in 1959 as if he had been a survivor he could have claimed the estate. As it happened, his sister died and the West German government had nobody to pay for the 600 acres of land, which went unclaimed.

Mother also told me they had Russian prisoners in their village during the First World War. They always said that they were good workers on the farm. She taught me to count in Russian to ten. This I still remember to this day.

Within a short time Alwin made Hauptfeldwebel. He used to come to us on vacation when his mother had moved to the city. On the street to our house were new army barracks. I liked to go with Alwin along here and he had a really good uniform and a long sword. All the soldiers had to salute him. I had to write letters to him which I did not like much and I knew I would never be in the infantry. Later he gave me his parade bayonet and an army flashlight with Red and green light. My father went to his wedding in East Prussia. He got a good pair of army boots as Alwin had become a store manager. I wore the Jack-boots for many years and later on I also got all his uniforms which were of really good quality. I climbed trees with the uniform on and it did not last long for me.

I also had a helmet and a South African hat. The hat was from the Lettov Vorbeck South African Corps. One day in the garden I had the helmet up. Along came the glazier. This was a man that replaced broken window glass. He talked me out of the helmet. He said he would turn it in at the barracks but I never got it back.

Several times I set fire to some bushes. People didn't know who had done it. In the bush one part was pine about 15 to 20 years old. I climbed the first tree and swung till I could reach the other one. I did this from one to the other, did not touch ground till the other end. 300 meter. I liked this time it was just good fun.

Mother said one time they were delivering a load of hay to the Army magazine. As Belgard had a garrison artillery, when passing the Kreishans city and surrounding seat, an attack by a Communist truck with a machine gun took place. They wanted to take over. Apparently they did not manage and they were driven off. It was Lieutenant Leber and his gang. Later in years, passing the Kreishans I looked at the bullet holes.

One time, I was at a big fair in the city on the midway where there were all kinds of games. This was about 1939 in the summer. I tried my luck on one of the wheels. I saw there were lots of good things I wanted. I turned the wheel and I had won top prize. For some reason, I had gone to this fair in the Hitler youth uniform. As soon as I had the top prize, a man in the middle started yelling again “a big win”. With this, he grabbed a picture of Hitler, 4 to 8 inches in size, claimed that was the top prize and I being in uniform could not refuse. Usually you had your choice on his table for top prize. I would not have taken the picture. But what could I do in uniform in May 1939? Everyone went to the city for the Mayday parade. It started with the S.A. and the flags which had to be saluted. After that came the S.S., just a few tall men, not too many. People knew what they were. Then followed other organizations, bands, flags, then the intelligencia. After that the trades. the workers, everyone marched in his class. This was always a big event and had to be seen.

Also, one day a year, the army opened the barracks gates to everyone. This I liked. I could see how soldiers were living. At the end, they gave us free “Erbsen” (peas) and “speck min bockwurst” (bacon with sausages) from the field kitchen. This was delicious – just superb- the best because the sauce made the taste. Just great, everybody had Erbsen with Speck and Bockwurst.

Once a year, the old Germans had some event celebrating the Summer Solstice. The Nazi party refreshed this costume. While I was still young, I did not have to go during the first years. In the evening we watched from our house and we were able to see the bonfires all around us. Later, I had to be there and sing and listen to speeches. In the end, the young people jumped over the nearly burned out flames. This was not done with fire during the war. At the end of the war, bonfires were all around us again. This time it was blazing houses in 1945.

In the summertime, everyone biked to the local lakes. One lake was very popular. It was not too far off the street (6 km). It had a nice beach and good clear water. Every 4 years, this lake claimed one life. One year, I think it was 1936, it was a young girl from our village. It was the Rostower See. When we had trips with the Hitler Jugend (Hitler Youth) which we did the year before the war, we stopped over in a Jugendherberge. These were youth hostels, built by the state in convenient locations with a building to watch over the area. For this, every schoolchild paid 1 pfennig or 12 pfennigs per year.

Sometimes when I came home with mother late in the evening from the farmer, she showed me where all the different stars in the sky were, like the great bear, the little bear. Casseopeia (7 stars). Then she showed me a ring around the moon one night. She told me with that, a change in the weather within 3 days. She was always right. In the winter, she feared the east wind. She claimed it came from Russia and was awful cold. We used to put straw mats in front of the windows.

One year, we were reading in the paper that 5 children had been born to a woman in Canada and all had survived. Mother told me about this at length. Canada at that time was not even a place on the map. I had no idea where Canada was. It was miles and miles away. Years later, I think it was 1955, I worked in Canada at a service station and a man asked me if I had ever heard of the Dionne Quintuplets. I had, and recalled what mother had told me years before in a different world when they were born. Then the man said, one of them died yesterday. This time I was only a few hundred miles from their place in Callander, Ontario.

Every year mother kept 2 goats. They gave some milk and we used the manure for the garden. These animals were as stubborn as a jackass or even worse. There was nothing you could do with them. Just plain stubborn. I had to take the young ones to the city. I got 25 or 30 pfennings for one. This money I could keep. Sometimes I helped the man on the railway crossing shining has lamps and his Morse telegraph. While he was on the railway line, he did not have the local paper, he had the Pommerische Zeitung (Pommeranian Newspaper). It was full of politics, no local news. He knew I was delivering the local paper and he wanted me to change my parents to the political papers. They never did. One day, they announced the golden book would come to our village. Here you could give money and sign your name in the golden book. It was laid out by this railway main in a house. I quite often had to do the newspaper collection on Sundays. You did the village in 2 hours. Most people gave 10, 20 or 30 pfennigs. One Sunday while doing this, the first one I came to gave me a 5 mark bill. I was not able to break this. I explained as I had just started. He made a point this is what he wanted to give. After this, giving changed as I spread the word one family had given 5 marks.

On Sunday afternoons, I usually went for a walk through the bush with my friends. It was not unusual to spot 30 deer in one day. All the local bush belonged to the next village Sidkow, which had 4000 hectares under the plough and 10000 hectares bush. This was by far not the biggest in the area. All the older villages had these estates. They had about 90 horses, 3 to a team, 3 to 4 tractors, 200 cows or more plus other livestock. The man in charge to the cows stopped in our village. He was called the Schroeizer and he had on the sign of his trade.

These estates had a castle for the baron or graf. These were the most common titles. Some were called ritters or rittergut (knights or good knight). The castles had 99 rooms. This way, he did not have to pay the room tax; 100 rooms or more and you had to pay tax. All the houses belonged to him, usually 40 or 50, and also the church. In his church, he had his own pew. It was a bit higher off the ground with a separate entrance. The baron was always able to look down on his people as help. Everybody whispered when the family came in. I went twice for church service in his church. He had a horse drawn carriage all enclosed with crystal glass windows and rubber tire wheels. The people in his village were very obedient to him. He owned them for a year. They were called Tagelohner. It means paid by the day. They could only move once a year or one certain day. I believe it was in February. Lots of horse drawn wagons passed by our house that day. They all thought they would be better off in the next village under a new master. When the baron came through our village in his carriage, we used to follow it and bother the driver as he was outside. We stood just outside of the reach of his whip. We did not have respect for a baron. Our parents were free of that. No service to any baron. I only worked a half day a year for them on the day of the hunt. This was in the winter. After school, most of the boys went to the hunt. Here, foxes and deer was usually what was hunted. In the evening, they wrote down your name and in a few days the forster (warden) from the Baron came in his splendid uniform with shotgun and he would thank you and pay 3 marks for being a helper.

The work on such a big estate was done quite rigidly to orders from the inspector. This inspector had agricultural schooling, usually university. He was the one who managed the estate for the baron. He never walked, always on horseback. He passed orders to the Hofmeister (Yard Master). He had to detail and put everybody to work. In the field, he hammered the ploughshare and people came out of their houses and marched along the street starting at one end and joined by others as he passed the houses. The evening before, he had been told where or which end of the village to start working. This Hofmeister always carried a heavy stick 8 feet long, his trademark. With his stick, he would point out everything. During the potato harvest he would poke the ground with it to see if he could find any buried potatoes.

Then there was the wagon master. He was in charge of the horses and to see that all the wagons were always in the right place. The cook for the Baron was called the Mamsel. A good one was just that – good. She was well known and was also allowed to cook for local weddings.

In the winter time in our area, the farmers used sleighs. They had sheepskin blankets and their feet in sheepskin bags. The horses had a blanket and bells. These bells sounded real nice. Sometimes I hitched a ride on a sleigh for a while. The cold drove you off for any length of time with no furs. Most winters I had frozen hands. In the spring it was awful, they just cracked up. One year I got a good salve from Doctor Griede. That one really helped. No more cracks or open hands after that.

It usually took a long time for spring to come in this area. It was usually connected with a flood of the Persante river. In the bushes by this river, the nightingales used to nest. To hear a nightingale in the summer evening is really the best. I have heard them for years and it was always delightful and new. In the early spring of 1939 one morning people were really excited. What they had seen the night before was a really big aurora. This northern light had started in the west according to some people moved to the north and east and got back to the north and died out really red in the east. Northern lights are not seen too often in this region and this one, so strong and seen by so many meant only war. Talk about this was around for weeks, as nobody knew that northern lights were common up north. With all the talk, war was not far away.

Mother usually raised one pig over the year. One year, this pig died. She went in the stall one afternoon and the pig quite sick. I had to go to the farmer who did and had everything illegal. He came and gave the pig a needle. It did not help. In the evening, the pig was dead. Father buried it the same night in the garden under that apple tree. Now mother remembered that she had let somebody in the stall and showed him the pig too. It was said that some people could put a hex on the pigs. These people were known through the grapevine talk. This person was put on that grapevine too often that nobody came into our stall anymore. No pig died after that anymore. A few weeks later we had another pig about the same size. There were no questions asked. It was from that farmer who did everything illegal.

In 1939, we finally got a radio. Father did not want one but mother kept needling him. He finally got mad one day, jumped on his bike and got a radio. 224 marks. 300 marks was the top you could pay so 224 marks was good. We surely liked this. As father was working, he did not qualify for a radio from the party for 99 marks. This was a radio the party would give you when you were considered poor. It was said they brought in the Deutschlandsender (Germany Channel) real clear and Hitler too. Several in our village received one.

One day our teacher had spotted an ad in the paper where it said the Volksvagen was on tour through Germany. It just so happened the street they came through passed right through our village. We waited on the side of the road and practiced "Anhalten" (calling cars to stop) all together. This worked quite well in rehearsal. When the cars turned up, everybody got so excited, they yelled anything. These were 3 black cars. Inside 2 S.A. uniformed chauffeurs. They stopped shortly, not for long. They had to be in the city for a show. The car was the first look I had at them. At that time, I did not even dream that I would buy my first one 15 years later in Canada. In the fall of each year after each harvest, the class went out on the Roggen (Rye) and wheat fields and picked them over again. One year the school had 800 lbs of extra Roggen (Rye). The whole school area one year had 1000 Zentener* of Roggen (Rye). This would otherwise have been lost. This work was called Ahrensammeln.

After we had picked it, it was put in bags and the bigger boys with bikes took it back to school, others had to walk. I usually had it on my back since I was one of the bigger ones. Once a year there was a big market in town. Everyone liked this. All children went right from school. The first two years in school, everyone had a slate plate to write on. On market day, this was usually left at home. Since there was not much thought about learning that day. When the lines on the slate were worn down, father got a straight edge and nail and just re-grooved them. It had to last 2 years.

All books for school were carried on your back. This was good and handy. In the winter, it was awful to go 1 1/2 kilometers to school, 2 feet of snow, 20 degrees below freezing. When we left the house just after 7 in the morning, mother told me how it was in the winter of 1928. Some trees froze. Another one of those winters was just ahead. This was the one of 1940-41. One day in the summer of 1939 we had a carpenter at our house. He showed father some figures. This was all that the Nazis had done on certain dates. He wrote this all down, added the numbers and the

* Zentener = 100 pounds. It is now a defunct unit of measurement

result was 1.9.39 or September 1, 1939. This he said, is the day the war will start. A Friday. And so it happened.

Father did not believe this. He had seen trains go behind our house for weeks. It was always said if the troops go the trumpenubungsplatz (trumpet practice grounds) it was a good, as this area was in that direction. In 1939, the troops had left earlier for their fall maneuvers. Goebbels was always on the radio. All the news contained cruel acts by the Poles to the Germans who were living there. In school, we had more politics. One morning, we heard on the 7 o'clock news that Germany and Russia had signed a pact to be friendly in the east. We told this to the teacher the first thing in class. He would not believe us. Next hour, he listened to the news and he heard it himself. He came back and we had to put the map of Europe up. Then he showed us what it could mean. Not much was done on this day. In the end, he said England discussed this pact with Russia and then Germany signed it. Roosevelt, President of the USA, he did not like it much so he made fun of him. The name Roosevelt sounds like a world full of roses in German.

Chamberlain, the Prime Minister of Great Britain was also made fun of too. As he always had an umbrella in most of his pictures, "Chamberlain and his umbrella, what does he want?" People were ignorant of the fact that climate and costumes were different in Britain. It would not have made any difference anyway, him and his umbrella.

In this year of 1939, there were 2 more events that I remember. Father had heard someplace that families with 3 children would get a baby bonus. One day he told us to stop by our Burgermeister (mayor) to get some forms. He filled them in and in no time, 10 marks arrived every month.

In 1939 on father's birthday, there was a big military parade in Berlin. We sat for hours by the radio and listened to the commentary of the parade transmitted over the "Deutschlandsender".

Sometime in the mid 1930's, a political group was established in the village by the Nazi party. They put up their own bulletin board and it was soon torn down several times. They finally picked a new location across the street from the shoemaker as he was home all day and worked at the window. He noticed who stopped and read all the bulletins. The glass of the bulletin box was reinforced with wire. After this, it was hard to vandalize.

One time all able men up to the age of 50 or so were informed to assemble in the local sporting grounds one Sunday morning. The reason for this was that a volunteer fire brigade was being formed for the village. My father was made commander of the brigade. Not much ever came of this as war was close.

One week in 1939 a "Lufschutzwoche" (air deference week) was declared. Everything had to be blacked out. All over Germany, planes flew overhead. They checked out how efficient it turned out to be. It was called off after about 5 days as it had turned out to be a complete success. All of this convinced people war was close at hand. Some bigger houses in cities had been marked by the signs "Luftschutzkeller" (air raid shelter).

As our village was not far from the Polish border, everybody knew for a long time that it had to come. In the last week of August, we heard that some people in our area had some packages or suitcases ready in case people had to flee from the incoming Polish army. My mother, after hearing this made 3 suitcases ready and they were in my room for a long time. I do not know what they had in there. I think it was some bedding and clothes. These 3 suitcases were supposed to hold our most valuable household items and support us for a while. Little did my mother know that she would not need these suitcases until 5 years later and then when she left, it was less than 3 suitcases full that she could take along. What a fate in thoughts. The last week in August in school, we discussed the Polish question every day and it got continually worse with propaganda. It heated up.

The city Belgard where I used to live was a garrison town. This means it had army barracks. On my way to work, I passed one every day. One morning in August 1939, the barracks square was empty and you heard no commands echoing over the square. I only saw a few soldiers around. Later in the day, I heard that the garrison had moved out that night. It would be 3 months till they returned. Their return was nothing like the time they moved out overnight. It was announced 2 days in advance the soldiers were returning. They de-trained around noon and drove through the city the long way. Horses were decorated, flags were flying, it was quite a day. A big celebration. A few days later, the soldiers had time off in the city. Some had decorations like iron crosses. The ones who had them were heroes of the town. Very quietly, the garrison got replenished and brought up to strength again. Their equipment looked like it had been in the war. Well, it had.

Also in the last week of August, it was announced that the Schleswig-Holstein school ship was on a visit to Danzig. We did not know anything of this as it was apparently for show to the people of Danzig. One week later we saw this ship in a German newsreel at the movie theater firing point blank into Polish bunkers and fortifications near Danzig. This ship isolated a strongly fortified Polish area and no damage was done to the city of Danzig by the Poles. As fate had it, I was near Danzig near the end of the war. Over my head, shells were flying from the Prince Eugen (ship). By the time I turned 18, I had lived in the mightiest nation on earth. I also had seen this same nation defeated and destroyed as no other nation ever before.

In years to come, I would see the mightiest nation on earth ruled by England and fall to pieces and England would just be left on its own. That's what Hitler did not want – the destruction of the English empire happening after his death. Such were the times I would live through.

Chapter Five: World War II

Friday September 1, 1939. We woke up this morning and we listened to the radio. As usual, it was marching music so we waited for the 7:00 a.m. news. During this, I heard the German army had already crossed the Polish frontier several hours ago. Not much detail came so far. Danzig was liberated as this had been a sore point in the propaganda all the weeks before.

On the 4th day in the morning, there was a loud roar in the sky. As I ran out of the house, I saw planes in formation of 3 just about right overhead about 700 feet high. I counted 18 bombers – 2 engine Heinkel 111's. This was the most planes people here had seen flying in formation. It was about 3 hours later and the planes returned in the same formation. After the 5th day of the invasion and from then on, the planes came over twice a day until the end of the fighting in Poland. One time on the way back we counted 17 planes and thought that one had been shot down. About 5 minutes later, the plane followed slow but intact. These 18 planes initiated quite a bit of talk as they came over so regularly.

Five years later, just about to the day in September 1944, I gave up counting 4 engine bombers. I had counted to 360 and then another bomber stream came into sight. At this time, I was with the 88 A.A. in Munich. While not everyone could count planes, we had appointed one of our men to count. He had come up with over 1000. There were 3 bomber streams of 360 planes each. In 1939, I was awed by 18-2 engine planes, but in 1944, I looked up and as far as I could scan the sky there were vapor trails of US bombers. There was nothing like it ever since. One time we were in Munich after a raid. The city smelled and stank of cordite explosives and the stench of dead people. Also fallen mortar and brick. The stench of dead people followed you everywhere. It was a relief to be back at the barracks after 3 days of such duty.

We left for school as usual. I remember we were sent home after the first hour. As Hitler was coming on the radio the same day, everybody listened to his speech. I can't say it made much sense to me. People in the village were uneasy. Everybody stood close to home. As usual, my father was called up some time ago. This time he joined the Luftwaffe (Air force). Ground personnel with him were others from out village and the area. By noon, the first real news came and the German troops were far into Poland already. We particularly watched the border near us and on Saturday, the second day, we knew we did not have to flee. On Saturday, I went to a farmer in the village to pick something up. By rights, he should have been in the army, but by good management and being at the right places, he was home.

He said to me, "The Germans were only making headway the first few days and what would happen when they got in to the mountains". I told him there were no mountains and the Germany army was already 100km into Poland. He did not say anymore. On Sunday morning, we heard that England had delivered an ultimatum in Berlin. We heard that England wanted all German troops pulled back. Lots of people at this time said the Germans should stop and peace should be made. The propaganda ran full blast on the Deutschlandsender and by noon we knew that England and France were in the war. My mother was very uneasy. She spoke of the blockade of 1914-1919 which we did not know much of. On the same day it was announced that all food and clothes would be rationed. Ration cards could be had by the local burgermeister (mayor) during the week. I remember we had ours the following Sunday and looked them over. On it were potatoes. We had a good laugh at this as we had potatoes by the truck load. Little did we know 5 years later we were not even able to buy a ration of potatoes for money. If you wanted some, you had to trade. Little else concerned us. We had our own chicken, meat-we had a pig, fruit and wheat we all grew on our own. I don't think we used the ration cards much in 1939 and 1940.

What was normal for a time each day was that we rolled out the map and followed the progress of the army. On the 5th day and from then on, things went really fast. We could see there was not much left of Poland. Every day the news had new surprises. It did not take long and someone in the village got around 20 Polish prisoners to do some work in the village. A day or two before Warsaw capitulated, the drama was at its height. March music was playing and then the Deutschlandsender told us to stand by for an important announcement. This went on for a while. Then it was announced that Hitler had offered Warsaw to surrender. Then followed an announcement in Polish; "owaga, owaga Warsaw" (attention, attention Warsaw). Then they said that they wanted it done by some hour. This was really well done propaganda. The whole thing was repeated every half hour in German and Polish.

From my father we heard a few weeks later that Warsaw had just been bombed to bits.

As my father had been called up before all of this had started, mother had found out where he was and how to get there. So one day, about the 10th of September, she put us in a taxi and off we went. Approximately 40 km to the field airport where father was stationed. As we got there about noon, we passed lots of military vehicles as we came close to the airport. We arrived just in time to see father board a big truck ready to drive off. He just said hello to us, had about 5 minutes with mother and he was gone. We did not go right home. I had a good look at all the planes. I saw fighters which were taking off and Heinkels that had some bullet holes. I was allowed to board a Heinkel. This airport had 4 buildings in a square just like a German farm, so from any airplane, it looked just like another farm. No concrete runway. My father wrote later he had moved to the airport in Warsaw (Oketszsky, Poland). He gave me the name of the rail line that he had travelled on. Four years later, I would travel this rail line too.

After Poland, things settled down. There was nothing going on in the west. I had lots of work. Whatever my father usually did at home, I now had to do. Cut grass for the goats, mess out the stalls, chop wood. I was busy.

One day at the end of September, within a day, a house in the village was fenced in with barbed wire and 20 Polish prisoners of war arrived. I had a look at the Poles. They looked just like us. Two could speak good German, some had blue air force uniforms, some just the brown coloured army uniforms. What we thought looked funny was the cap, diamond shaped on top.

The 2 German speaking ones were talking to us and one man said he was an artist. If we got him some crayons or coloured pencils, he would draw us a good picture. I mentioned this to my mother. I got some money and bought crayons. I handed these through the barb wire and the wired windows. Two days later I had 2 drawings. One showed a Polish ship being bombed by a German plane. Of course everybody liked it.

The apples were still on the tree and mother said to take some along to the prisoners which I did. I never liked the look of those hands coming through the wired windows. All this happened to the same house where the Russian prisoners had been in the First World War. While all this was going on with the prisoners, I had no idea I would be one myself in 5 years. At first the Poles did not work for about a week. We had a big swamp behind our village and it was said the prisoners would be sent to work to drain the swamp. This turned out to be true. One day I came home from school and there were 20 prisoners working digging a ditch. One guard was with them. I got a shovel from home and went over to where they were digging and started to dig too. It did not take long until the guard showed up and chased me away. I did not go back to them. Little did I know that I would be digging ditches. I would get my chance to dig ditches as a P.O.W. in England some years later. What an irony. The swamp the prisoners drained turned out to become a real good field. It grew top quality wheat.

One morning, school started and we were surprised to have what was a schedule. Here was the teacher giving us instructions on how to deal with prisoners or other Polish people which might show up. After this talk, nobody went near the prisoners anymore.

One time, he said papers had been found in Poland by the German army that showed maps of Poland with their western border being the river Oder. This was all the land we were living on. Then he made us imagine we were Polish and he picked some at random in class and they had to give their name in Polish. One I remember was called Winkel. In Polish, he called himself Winkelsky. We all had a good laugh at this but it made it clear what was going to happen to us when the war went the other way. As this was 1939, everyone was full of victory. What happened 5 years later was by far worse than we were ever taught in school in 1939. The newspapers still showed pictures from Poland and in some scenes the devastation and slaughter was absolute. The heading to all these pictures on the end of Poland was "MIT MAN UND ROSS UND WAGEN HAT SIE DER HERR GESCHLAGEN" (with man and horse and cart did the lord slay them). This is written somewhere in the bible.

All the time, I had lots of work as my father was still in Poland. In the new year, we had a talk one evening through the local railway line that my father was on his way back to his home base and he would pass through our town and there would be a stop-over. This call came from 2 hours train time down the line. We had a 1 hour walk to the station. Mother and I left at once and in little time, the train with my father arrived. This was quite a reunion. He had all kinds of stuff which he gave to us to take home. We had not expected this and I made an umbrella into a basket that was full of chocolate, vodka and cigarettes. We went home loaded.

Several days later, father came home for vacation for a week. He had a Polish rifle with him. This was for the local game warden. Then he had good cloth for a suit, an officer's air force cap, a map briefcase from a Polish officer, lots of tools, all kinds of things we could use. Also several bottles of real Polish vodka. Since we had lots of visitors at this time, everybody got a glass of vodka.

There was lots of talk about what he had experienced in Poland. One story was the best. This sergeant, a young professional soldier, used to carry scissors in his pocket while going out in Warsaw. This he used whenever he happened to see a Jew, then trimmed the beard of the Jew. They were not allowed to steal anything from the Polish stores, but he said control at the gate was only a token gesture as everyone went into Warsaw and helped himself. The cloth he had wound around his body and he put his greatcoat (overcoat) over top of it He passed the gate without incident. In 1941, I had a real nice suit from this for my confirmation.

A few weeks after my father went back to his unit, he wrote that he would be home soon as all the reservists were not needed anymore. He was released in the fall of 1940.

In 1940 I started my last year of school. It had been on and off for a long time. Teachers changed quite often. Twice a week, I now went to bible class in the city for instruction by the local pastor to get ready for confirmation. To carry books, I used the map case that father had brought from Poland. It was real handy.

The years 1940-41 were a good time in Germany. Every day, something new was on the radio. Then the German army went into France and Denmark-Norway. The latter we could not understand. It was said the English wanted Norway and the German army beat them by 10 hours. Everybody thought the Germans would lose this as the English fleet would just blast everything out of the water. This was not so. We heard of some German losses of ships but the loss of some 20 destroyers was not mentioned. My mother heard that through Radio London in German language. By the end of the French campaign, we sang in school, "Uber die Hass, uber die Schelde, und Rhein marchiren Siegrichnach Frankreich hinein" (Over the Mense, Scheldt and Rhine (rivers), we march victorious into France). Against England, the song was "Den wir fahren gegen Engeland (then we go towards England). For Africa, they had "Panzer rollen Afrika vor" (Tanks roll ahead in Africa).

As we had some people in our village who had escaped from the Bolsheviks in Russia after the revolution, my mother had become friendly with several families from there. She often visited their homes during the long winter evenings. As I was older towards the end 1930s, my mother took me with her. One family had a boy about my age. Several times, I listened to what the grown-ups had to talk about as politics were very much in the news at this time in Germany. One evening, my mother was able to get the other woman talking about her escape from the Bolsheviks and how they managed to reach this part of Germany. It was a fascinating story how the Bolsheviks herded people up in the night and deported them to Siberia. I also heard the hardships people had to endure after leaving their homes in Russia out of fear of being rounded up for deportation. I had no idea that I was listening to the future and it was not that far away as the Russian army and communists came to these parts of Germany in 1945.

The stories of the escape from the Bolsheviks were repeated again in the real. Whoever could move, moved on towards the west. Everyone had heard the horror stories from the East. It was no better in 1945 than it had been during the Russian revolution. People trembled when they heard name from Russia and these people were partly the first to pack up and start to move towards the west. As before in 1920, they still had no place to go. In 1945, fear just moved them out. As it turned out, the communists in 1945 who came to our region with the Red Army, had names of the people that escaped from Russia. Whoever they found in 1945, had seen the last sunrise the day they were found.

As my mother believed everything she had heard from these folks and the Red Army came nearer to our village, my sister did not need much convincing to make her leave, even though it meant leaving absolutely everything behind, that she had worked for in her lifetime.

Above: The Gutzke family at Manfried's confirmation in 1941 Left to right: Charlotte, Martha, Max, Manfred and Dora in front. (Roy Gutzke Collection)

During the winter of 1940, the soldiers were always in town. In the early spring, some units disappeared and in a few weeks, the barracks had gone quiet again. Over a period of time, they had moved out to the west.

The French campaign had been followed with great interest by everybody and when the troops were past Paris, everyone relaxed. By now, it could not happen again like in 1914. Every day there were special bulletins in the air and it was not long until it was announced that France was suing for peace. When France capitulated that day, our city put on a big parade with the remaining soldiers in town. Everybody was very jubilant. What I witnessed was the absolute glory of the 3rd Reich. There were fireworks, parades, flags, speeches and extra ration coupons. The 3rd Reich was at its highest point in its short binge. From the time I saw that France parade to the end of the war, I would have a turbulent time. I did not know at this time that this was the last parade I would see with German soldiers and the last time I would see a city bedecked in Swastika flags. Next time I saw a city in flags, they were white. The troops on the move through town by motorized units were Americans. This was the low point of the 3rd Reich. A few days later, the surrender was signed.

Italy was Germany's ally. One day, our teacher showed us a map of Italy. He said this could easily be defended because it was only 200km wide. This proved to be correct only 3 years later. Nobody had heard of large amphibious landings on the rear of enemy troops so he did not include this, but on defense, he was absolutely right.

I left school in the spring of 1941. My reference paper was good as we had our old teacher back for a while after the fall of

France. We really learned a lot from him these past months.

In April of 1941, I started to go to work for a merchant in town. He had “Lebensmittel and “Eisenwaren” (this was groceries and hardware) plus a big yard with stalls for horses and wagons. He also had beer, wine and liquor. I applied for this position on my own. I had a simple test, some arithmetic and some writing. Just like my life, this was a usual procedure and more or less a formality that you knew something. At the end of my life history I wrote that in March of 1941, I was incorporated into the Hitler Jugend (youth). This last sentence was really it. My future boss nearly had a fit. He said he was not interested if I was in the Hitler youth. He walked out talking to himself. I was hired anyway.

The firm was “Karl Rakow Belgard Wilhem Str. AG”. The owner was with the “death head Husars” during World War One. He still had some mementos from the Husars in his living room. He had what looked like a big fur hat with a big tin skull at the front of the hat. I looked at this quite often and little did I know that 3 ½ years later, I would wear a hat with a skull on the front. The cap of the SS troops.

Chapter Six: Jungvolk, Hitler Youth and Joining the SS

Now I will talk about my time in the Jungvolk and Hitler Youth from 1937 to 1944.

The Jungvolk, which was also called pimple, was for boys 10 to 14. You had duty 2 times each week in the evening for games and songs. Saturdays and Sundays, it was 3 to 4 hours for some exercise, sport, marching and talk of the Nazi party and Hitler. You had a uniform, short pants, brown shirt and a cap, shoes and socks at discretion. Then a tie and leather knot belt, shoulder belt and a knife after you have passed some tests. You had to have camped out for a few days and know how to pack your gear. To keep track of what you had done, you had your personal book where everything was recorded. For example: if you attended a 3 day trip or what you had accomplished each year in sport; also promotions. You had to pay (35 pfennig) for this book. Also, there was a fee of 10 pfennig per month. This was always a pain for my father to pay. He sure did not like it. I only got the money after asking several times over several days. My time in the Jungvolk was a fiasco to start with. For 2 days, I was a "Hordenfuhrer". It meant actually nothing. You were in charge of 3 other youths. The next step was "Jungenshafsfuhrer" in charge of 9 to 12 boys. Then it went to 30 and then 120. The 120 unit was called a "Fohulsin". To be in charge of this unit was quite a lot. You were only there about a year because when you turned 14, the Hitler Youth took you. In general, the Jungvolk was not much. You were in it, that was absolutely all. In one 2 day camp, we were feeding from an army field kitchen and our mess tin. This was fun to us. Just a taste of things to come. I would later get a mess tin from the army.

From the age of 14, the Hitler Jugend (H.J.) took you in. Here were youths up to the age of 18, so all the kid's stuff was gone. You had your choice in this and that of what you wanted to join. You could pick your future profession. If you wanted to be a fireman later in life, you joined the Fire H.J. A mechanic would join the Motor H.J. A flyer would join the Glider H.J, and a rider had the horses. Even a musician could go to the "Musikcorp" H.J. You had your choice. The uniform was all the same; black pants, brown shirt, armband with a swastika and belt knife. There, you could earn all kinds of badges and stripes on your sleeve.

The rank started with "Rotenfuhrer". He was in charge of 3. Next, "Kameradshaftfuhrer)" in charge of up to 12. Next, the "Shar", up to 30. Next, as rank only, "Hauptsharfuhrer". The next unit a Gefolgshaft. This was 3 "Shars" or about 120 youths. Identification was a green and white lanyard and at least a star. Pip on the shoulder. This was quite a rank, "Gefolgshaftfuhrer". There was about one for every 3 to 4 villages. It depended of course on the population. The next rank was "Stamm" with a white lanyard which was 3 to 4 "Gefolgshafts". This was not a boring rank as it was nearly a full time job. Next, the "Bahnfuhrer". This was a full time job with office and the Hitler Youth paid you, usually a young ex-army officer. You wore a red lanyard. Duty was usually 2 times per week. One evening or weekends in the city with other units in sport competition.

There was absolutely no smoking in uniform, no unruly behavior in uniform. You had to salute all elders you knew which were in the party, police, army N.C.O. and officers.

The Hitler Youth was more active in sports competitions where you had to jump, run and throw a ball a certain distance for your age. You had to have 185 points to earn a badge for the year. The first year I didn't make it but I did make it later. I threw the leather ball 40 meters, a record for my age. That throw pulled me out of the competition. I went on 2 trips for 3 days which was very useful. One trip was to the village where the devil had wrecked the church. On one trip I was not supposed to go. I took the bike and went anyway. My mother gave me nothing to eat. Some 20 km down the road the leader of the group learned I had no food. He biked up to me and asked if I was supposed to be on the trip. I said yes I was. As I did not want to leave my parents, then how come I had nothing to eat? I told him we were poor and there wasn't much food in the house. He said Hitler Jungend are comrades and I got to eat from everyone and the problem was solved.

While we were shooting with an air rifle in the Jungvolk and at times in the Hitler Youth, this now changed to a 22. Single shot, Mauser action. Before you were allowed to shoot, you had to know all the parts of the 22. The first year was usually slow as the older ones moved out. You were in line for a rank the second year. The first year in the Hitler Youth, I didn't advance, just did what I had to do and be alright in sport. I got my sport badge that year. Ball throwing had changed to what we call a "Keule". This weighed about 1 ½ pounds. A steel ring on top of a wooden handle. The second year, I went to a camp for 2 weeks. This was about 150 km from home. Here we were over 1000 Hitler Youths. This was in tents in the summer of 1942, near the Baltic Sea. The place was Peenemunde. We had no idea what was going on here. We saw funny planes coming near with short wings and hardly a propeller. The planes had something on top near the rear and the noise from this plane was not like anything we had ever heard. One time, one crashed or exploded only 300 to 400 meters from our camp. It was a really big blast. This camp was in the outskirts of Peenemunde, in other words, a buffer zone. We of course, all loyal Hitler Youth, were allowed in here. Sometimes, we travelled to the base. There was nothing to see, just a few houses, vehicles and lots of trees. The planes coming over us would be called the V-1.

This camp was quite good for me. I learned to do lots of things on my own. Mother was not here to look after me. I also learned a lot concerning the Hitler Youth. On the 4th day, we learned that each Gefolgshaft would get an N.C.O. from the army as a trainer. This was in 1942. The N.C.O arrived the very next day. From now on, things changed. It was more field training now than sport and games. We got up at 6:00 am and started with a mile run. Then we had until 7:30 to get the tent cleaned up, wash and have breakfast. We were 12 to a tent and I liked this time. Only 3 years later, I hated the sight of a tent. After breakfast, we had some exercise. Practice shooting went fast from noon as it was one hour afterwards. The food was good but we were always hungry. It was explained to us that we had more to eat in this camp than the ordinary German outside. It was just the fresh air near salt water and lots of running around that made us hungry. I guess it was true. We had enough to eat.

The next little village was 4 km through the bush. On the way in, I had seen a bakery. I had some ration coupons and I went to the bakery one night and got 2 loaves of bread. I was told he could not accept those coupons, but he knew we were hungry and

I would get my 2 loafs of bread. It did matter little as it was only a few days till the end of our stay. As the N.C.O. came in, we asked him what those funny planes were. He knew less than we did as we had seem them at the base where he was not allowed. The riddle was solved 2 years later. This funny plane was called the V-1 or "Buzzbomb".

The trip back was real nice. First by rail to Peenemunde, then on a ship to Stettin. From the ship, we saw the big plants along the Oder River. It was called the Politz. This was where we made gasoline from coal. The plant was surrounded by balloons. There were also heavy anti-aircraft batteries around. Stettin itself was a lovely very nice city. Also, no bombs had fallen here yet. From Stettin home by train, 140 km, was good all through nice pine forest. At times we saw the street which was near the rail line. There was not much traffic on the street. In the spring of 1945, I travelled through the same area and what a difference. At home in the Hitler Youth, I had come back from a 2 week camp. A promotion followed to "Kameradshatsfuhrer" with a red and white lanyard from the pocket to buttonhole on the shirt and I was in charge of 10. After this, I made the shooter's badge and next year's sport's badge again. Then, one day, I heard that those one year older than I was, had been to a 3 week camp called a "Kreigsubungslager". Here they had received uniform and all was in military style. He informed us that this camp was really tough. While this had just started in 1942, you got nothing out of it compared to later. In 1943, it was my turn for one of these 3 week camps.

In 1943 when I came back from a camp set up by the Hitler Youth from Peenemunde, the trip was by ship through the inland lake named Stettin Hoffsee and up the Oder River to Stettin. I had been to this city several times before. Here, I heard that in the town parade square (I knew where it was) there was a Russian T34 Tank on display. Of course I walked over and had a good look at it. I did not find it as good looking as the German Panzer IV and certainly by far, not as good. To prove my point, it had 2 holes in its armour where German guns had gone in and disabled it. What I did not know then and would not have believed anyway, was that I was looking at the best tank that came out of the war. Wide tracks, sloped armour, good gun, easy to take care of. Towards the end of the war, it would be a real menace to the Wehrmacht because it was so plentiful and by that time, handled by well experienced tank crews. A year and a half later, I would face these T34s in battle with an 8.8 flack gun. What happened there was that we had more tanks than we could handle. Their experienced crews just looked us over and within a short time, we were overrun. After the war, I did some research to see who that was that we had faced. That particular Russian tank division that I faced later in the war was one that Stalin had elevated to a guard division a week before they ran into us. The elevation to guards division was on account of their heroic fights and breakthrough through the German lines. They deserved it. When they overran us, I counted about 30 tanks, then I gave up. I have never seen so many. Needless to say, I only had my mind set on getting away from them, which in the end, I was able to. A few months later, these T34 tanks, would capture the city of Stettin and stay there. As Germany had lost the war, Stettin was given to Poland by the leader of the state of East Germany, at that time a good communist who had escaped from the Nazis in the 1930s to Moscow. Now in 1945, he returned to rule East Germany. As a present, he gave Stettin to Poland. Actually, the river Oder was to be the border, which we had heard in 1940 in school from the Polish prisoners in Germany. Poland would go to the Oder after the war. We all had a good laugh at this. as the Wehrmacht at this time was by far the strongest army in Europe if not the world. In the summer of 1940, it would overrun France in 6 weeks, so nobody believed what the Polish POWs were telling us.

*To my son Roy: at the age of **16** years. I volunteered for the duration of the war to join the Waffen SS unit of the German army in the National Socialist country under the leadership of Adolf Hitler. What I did not know at **16** years of age that was the Waffen SS units were the roughest toughest hardest fighting units which ever walked on this earth. There is no denying of this fact and history has been written on it. By the time I was 18 years of age, I had been to hell and back not once not twice but enough for a lifetime. The man who says he is not afraid during a war facing the enemy has not been born yet. Such a man is not around to talk about it. Death has claimed him.*

In the spring of 1943 we had a big meeting in the city this was called Stammapell. This we heard of about 2 weeks in advance. Everybody had to be there. It started in the afternoon. We saw a movie from the glorious and victorious German army it was from all units of the armed forces. After this somebody talked to us. By now it was late in the afternoon. We were told to line up in our shorts. 30 youths. I was in the front line. We had no idea what was going on or what was going to happen. I was 16 so were most others some were 17. There were no 18 year olds because they were already in the army. While I was standing there I remember a young very nice looking N.C.O. from the Waffen SS approached me. He had several medals like the Iron Cross and others. He had a very nice field grey uniform. In fact I had only seen one man in a Waffen SS uniform once before and he was it. I followed him for a while and admired him. How he walked and how he said that he had served in the SS as we had heard about the SS at times in our region. But no SS was stationed near us. This N.C.O. from the Waffen SS asked me if I ever had in mind joining the Waffen SS. I told him outright, "no!" as I would join the 88 anti-aircraft and I had not heard that the SS had anti-aircraft. When he heard this he told me that the Waffen SS had 88 anti-aircraft and if I volunteered today, I would be sure that I could join what I volunteered for. Whereas if I was drafted to the army I could end up any place.

After hearing this I volunteered right away. When I was called up in 1944 I found out this N.C.O had been true to his word. I was assigned to the 88 flak. After volunteering I looked for a friend of mine, the son of the Burgermeister (mayor) of the village. I motioned him to join me and it was only a minute later and he did so too. We were the only ones which joined and volunteered for the Waffen SS from all the villages around. I did not say anything about this at home. I did not think it was important as I had to go to the army anyway. It only took my mother until next day to find out. The son of the Burgermeister was scared stiff by what he had done. He went straight home after we had the medical right there and then told his father the Burgermeister he was in the SS. The Burgermeister was a party member that's why he was Burgermeister in the first place. When he heard his son was in the Waffen SS and I had more or less been responsible for it, he raised hell with everyone. My mother heard about it and the Burgermeister never forgave her. In 1944 she wanted some apples from him to give to me, but she never got them. It would have been wrong for her to complain to higher ups and the Burgermeister would have ended up in a camp if he did. My mother never said anything but she did not forget.

The next day the Burgermeister went to all the local offices in the army to get his son out of the SS. It was absolutely useless.

He accomplished nothing. I never knew why he did not want his son in the SS as he was a party member and should set a good example. Not long after his son was called up in 1944 and sent to Prague, Czechoslovakia. I don't know which unit he ever joined because he never talked to me after this day. It just proved one thing. The Burgermeister was not able to get his son out as he was told the signature of a 16 year old was absolutely binding in this case.

In the fall of 1943 I was called to a Wehrertuchtigunglager. This was for 3 weeks in Lauenburg about 100km east of us near the former Polish border. The place used to be an insane asylum, but the insane had been taken care of by then. The party had one rule. If you had to be supported by the state and no chance of getting better you were disposed of by an SS doctor. This news leaked out as some people had some family in Lauenburg in the asylum and they got informed that they had died there. So many was no coincidence. Some said it was a blessing.

Part II: Life in the Wartime SS

Chapter Seven: Training in the 2nd SS Toten Koft Division

The 30 buildings that made up the asylum in Lauenburg was all in a lovely forest really well built and equipped. After all the insane were gone the SS had taken over and trained their future N.C.O. here. While I had volunteered for the SS it was no coincidence that I went to a Wehrertuchtigunglager under SS training. The SS trainers were N.C.O.s from the SS Toten Kopf Division (Dead Heads Division) #2 and discipline was straight. We were quartered in 2 buildings. Duties were hard but then only for the first 3 days. 10P.M. was lights out at times the N.C.O. checked soles of your feet when you were in bed. God help you if they were not clean. Since we were all young and very active, we were told the SS N.C.O. in the complex gave some of their food to our kitchen and we had plenty to eat. Never at any time was I hungry in this group. You could say they looked after their own. At the end of 3 weeks I had made Schiesswart and this entitled me to wear a band on my left sleeve Shiesswart. In other words I could conduct a shooting match with the Hitler Jugen under my command as I had command of 30 of them by now. I liked this camp so much I informed the top instructor that I would like to come back for another 3 weeks. He wasted no time - after one week I was back. In such cases the mail worked absolutely perfectly. In the 2nd 3 week period I made Kriegsubungsletter (war instructor) finished first in a class of 150. I was allowed to wear another band on my left sleeve. Both titles were secret yearnings of everybody in the HJ. I made both in 6 weeks, plus jumped some ranks up.

None of the other boys in my village had ever accomplished this. By now nobody could tell me anything anymore. My sleeve bands spoke a good language. There was only one higher rank which meant nothing to me. I came back for my 2nd 3 weeks and so as word got around what I accomplished and I had top rank in this, I received a 22 caliber rifle, ammunition and a book from shooting matches. The shooting matches only recorded on paper the ammunition I used for hunting hares or shooting doves. I was not allowed to hunt, but it did not bother me one bit because when I wanted a hare or Partridges, I went out and shot one. One hare I remember was in the grass a distance of about 40 meters I could only see his ears and head. I fired and saw him jump, I thought I had missed and had run off. I never moved after that shot for some time. Someone could have heard the shot and when he started looking nothing moved so they usually figured there was nothing. So I went to the place where I had seen the hare and he had dropped where he stood. I had shot him right through the eye at a distance of 40 meters.

On another day I saw a sparrow on the telephone line. I fired at him and down came the line. It did not bother me. Next day a man in a post office uniform came to the store where I worked. I had seen him before and he knew me. When everybody had left the store he said he had found a shot through the wire not far from where I was living at home and he knew I had a rifle. This would cost 120 marks for lost telephone calls, plus the repair. It was the line between 2 cities' 150 KM apart. I heard all this and asked him who knows about all this. I found it was just him and he had just blamed it on the wind breaking an old line. He had this all figured out even before he came to our store because he asked me for 2 Lbs. of sugar without coupons. I gladly gave him his 2 lbs. It didn't come out of my budget. This sugar disappeared real fast under his coat and he never bothered me after. Nothing was mentioned at home about me shooting the wire. Whenever I shot a hare I had to go to Grandmothers house and skin it as mother wanted no evidence around our house just in case. Nothing ever happened and I was happy hunting. In looking back I had found that going to the camps had been beneficial to me. Everything was free and I saw other areas of the country. One time I was at a 3 day camp near the lake, which claimed a life every 4th year. On the first day we had noodles boiled in water. Nearly everyone dumped them in the lake, even the fish did not eat them.

In rank I was as high as I wanted to be in a short time. I had 2 sleeve strips which were good. On the day at the Streifendienst, some were given the name H.J. Streifendienst. This meant like roving duty or patrol duty. This was not much. It was kind of identification for higher authorities of the ones who had signed for the Waffen SS so we were not bothered by any of this. In fact, as soon as you had signed you were free from all the other nonsense. The Streifendienst went on patrol with a policeman from the city as no one under the age of 18 was allowed to be on the street after 10pm. unless he was in company of an adult. I went to the movies, which finished after 10pm, on the way out there was the policeman and the Streifendienst. They stopped me as they knew I was not 18. In the end the policeman came over, asked me what I had volunteered for and I told him the Waffen SS. I was let go at once. This cleared me once and for all. No Streifendienst bothered me after 10 pm.

One time in the winter of 1943 I had to go to the barn that was the higher H.J. office. I needed more ammunition for my shooting. Here the leader saw me he wanted to know how I had been doing. I told him. At the end he asked me if I wanted to go to another camp. I was for it. He did not say anymore and I forgot about it. Then one day the end of March 1944 I had a letter with rail tickets and a 3 week pass to a camp in Czechoslovakia. This was really good because it was a spa where we did nothing for 3 weeks. I found out it was for all H.J. boys who achieved something and this was the thanks.

On the way down on the overcrowded trains I stood on one leg from Dresden to Prague for almost 2 hrs. The train was full. It was really good we walked through the bush, the mountains and visited Prague the capital of Czechoslovakia for 3 days. Pilsen was its beer. Food was as much as we wanted. No duties and maids cleaned the rooms. This was a new hotel and the only guests were Hitler Youths. For 3 weeks it was 120 boys then 3 weeks 120 girls. It was the absolute best for free.

The trip back had a layover in Berlin. Here I had a distant relative, we called her Aunt Heta. I visited her while I walked around Berlin. I saw a funeral that must have been for some higher officer in the army because there were all kinds of officers with lots of decorations and Knights cross with swords in black Mercedes cars. I don't know who got buried as this went by pretty fast. Berlin was still in good shape. Only the odd house or building was damaged. It was still a city full of life.

After I came home I organized the local Sport fest of the H.J. This was a big event. I invited several teachers from the villages to add the points, plus some other officials. It was a fine day and we did well. To organize and do a Sport Fest was the highlight of my career in the H.J. After a dismal start. I had come a long way. This was my first Hitler Youth Sport Fest I organized and was in charge of. Unknown to me and all the participants it would also be the last sport fest held because by the time May 1945 came around the 3rd Reich and all its organizations would be a pile of rubble and most of its leaders were dead. The Hitler youth was outlawed and disbanded.

During the war years marks were given by points. At first we had several young boys who would reach over 300 points. During the war years it declined to the best of 280 points. The best of the Hitler youth were in the Wehrmacht or Luftwaffe and few had survived by 1944.

To do the Sport fest in the Hitler Jugend and organize it was always a big event and honor to the local H.J. In 1944 I had the honor as Gefolgschaftsfuhrer in charge of 150 youths 14 to 18 years of age. In 1944 the sport fest was still good even though it was somewhat subdued and not festive. On the end gefolgschaftsfuhrer which was me this year said a few words and closed the sport fest. I had a speech prepared thanking the officials and the helpers also I had to mention our victorious army. I was going to say our victorious army is fighting in the desert in Africa to the snows of the Nortcap in Norway, in front of Leningrad in the Russian steppes on the Volga at Stalingrad and on the Atlantic. Looking this over and reading it, I realized it was all wrong by 1944. The Africa Korps was buried in the sands of the desert or taken prisoner, Norway was of no interest, in Leningrad the blockade had been broken by the Red Army, the Russian steppes held the graves of the 6th German Army from Stalingrad and no German soldier was at the river Volga anymore. People talked about an Allied invasion which everybody expected to come very soon. With all this I had very little to say.

I had my call up papers in my pocket for the 6th of June which was in 2 days' time. When I left that day my mother told me in the morning the invasion had started by the Allies on the beaches of Normandy. Nearly to the day 11 months later May 8 1945 the war would be over in Europe the Hitler Jugend Sport Fest a thing of the past and not remembered. When war broke out in 1939, I was 12 years old and we counted the years as boys we figured 4 years of war so we would not be in it. We were wrong. The disaster in Stalingrad in 1943, in Africa, to the Kursk battle and in the Russian steppes had depleted the once mighty Wehrmacht. In the summer of 1943, all the boys in the Hitler Jugend 16 years of age were commanded to appear in a big rally in the city. Here after some speeches you were asked and ordered to sign up for the army. By your 17th birthday you were called up. I was lucky. My age by call up was 17 and 2 months. For a few months' time boys would be called to the army younger than 16.

At the beginning of war there were already special bulletins of victories by the Wehrmacht or Navy. For example: the radio would play marching music as it said that U-Boat 47 in Scapa Flow sank a battleship. These bulletins would not stop until April 1945. After that the RAF and the 8th US Air Force had no more targets of opportunity in Germany. These bulletins sounded different. For example they said, "Berlin: enemy bombers over Brainschhoeg-Hanover in direction of Berlin" so it was day after day, Berlin had 230 days of bombs during the war.

While I had been away in 1944 my mother said I had some mail at home. It looked to her like the call up letter to the Reichsabeitsdienst (labor Service) and she sent it back. I looked into this and found it was the call up and it would be mailed again in time. I closed most of my books with the H.J as I would be away from home for 3 months. The 22 rifle I turned over to my successor in the next village. As this rifle had a plaque on the butt from Innsbruck and it had been there as one in my group had earned the title Meistershutze (Master shooter). This was one grade better as the top order Sharpshooter. He was the best in the H.J. in Pomerania in Innsbruck and he achieved 16 best H.J shooter titles in Germany. His name was Heinz. Not too many people knew about me passing the rifle on as our tenant Emil John lost his life over it one year later. He was asked and they assumed he knew where the rifle was, however he did not know.

One time I came home from the H.J duty in the evening and in the living room was Emil John and my father with the ear to the radio. They had radio Moscow on which transmitted every night in German at 10pm it was called the paradise of the workers. But nobody wanted to live there. Stalin scared every one. It was so funny here, I was in the H.J uniform and my father listens to the Communist broadcast. At the end of the broadcast he always turned the dial away from that station's static.

Now I will have to go back to where I started to work for Herr Rakow in Belgard. This place was well known as it had everything from food to drink to nuts and bolts. Just about anything anybody would ever want. Business was best Saturdays and Mondays as all farmers came in on Mondays for the hog or pig market, which happened every Monday. Business hours were from 8 am to 12 noon and from3 to 7pm. From noon to 3pm we were supposed to be closed, but the front door was locked and the back door wide open, but we were officially closed. It was an 11 hour day. I found it hard at first and just dropped at night. Here I was to train for 3 years this included business school twice a week, which I did not like at first. It was a bit much for me at first as I had come out of a village school with lots of missed time on account the teacher being away. One day in the fall I had a letter at home from the local labor office to drop in for an interview. I did so and the man there was surprised to see me in a business attire as his records showed I did not do the required one year land year (work on a farm) after I had left school. This was the law at the time that all 14 year olds had to do one year on the land. He showed I had not. With this news I went back to the store and told them what was up.

It just so happened that one of the regular employees from the Labour office was our customer who used to drop in at times to drink. He had seen me at his office that day while I was being interviewed. On top of being our customer he had been re-schooled to a civil service position from bricklayer. The time he had been a bricklayer he had worked with my father and they were buddies from away back and really good friends. What happened now was stronger than any law the Nazis could make. He said I know his father I am his friend and I enter him in the books that he is on the farm and you keep him here at the store. It was as simple as that. Settled the same day and sealed with some drinks from a Schnapps bottle. He did not care if he got in trouble with the Nazis. He was Max's friend. That was it. So I stood where I was. I did not go to school till next April when I started there again officially. It worked out fine. Then next April I started in school again and I liked it. Work was easier by now too. Since there was no pay for apprentice for the first 2 years I received 30 marks a month the last year, which they did not have to give me. I did a good job and 30 marks was 10 marks better than my predecessor had received.

The food was good. Some of our customers owned a butcher shop and things changed hands. By now at the beginning of 1941 everything was rationed, the storekeepers had a lot horded which they had not declared for coupons.

I found a cellar always locked and a room upstairs in the house that was always locked. It did not bother me the first year. I had my own customers for trading with schnapps and schnapps was plentiful. The year after I became top man as the others who were older got called up to the military. By this time schnapps had nearly run out. I had bottles hidden all over the cellar and in the end I had more than the owner himself so I thought. In 1940 this store had become a member store organized with the K.D.F Kraft durch freude (Strength through Joy). It displayed a swastika on a sprocket wheel. This was the only organization I belonged to outside of the H.J. The store had 12 full time employees and extra help on top of the 12 so it applied to the KDF. This KDF took over all labour unions in 1933. We had good perks through this organization. Low priced theater tickets, trips to Kolberg in the Baltic Sea, where I saw a man performing being electrocuted on stage. This was big drama as electricity was not known to everybody as it is now. It was a good gruesome show. The K.D.F also had 4 large ships to take members for a small fee like 12 marks on 2 week trips to other countries like Norway, Spain and some islands. Not to England though as these ships were not allowed by England to dock there. Apparently the English did not want to let English workers see how German workers were living under Nazism. I talked to one who had been to Norway and he really enjoyed it.

As the owner was an old Kaisertrener loyal to the Kaiser he did not like the Swastika sticker much on the windows. He was not asked - it was there and that was that. It showed that the firm was unionized. Every fall he went to a spa for his health. He always claimed he had heart problems, which in the end turned out to be right. He just dropped dead one day and that was it.

There was nothing new about this death as the former owner of the store dropped dead too (the one who had built and owned the store first). There was a hex on the building so it was said by older folks who had known all the previous owners. This could not be disputed as things really had happened that way. After all these years it would interest me if the owners are still dropping dead. As the Scnapps ran short and out for trading, I started to look at the locked doors and what I found in the cellar made my eyes bulge. It was the private storeroom of the boss. He had a good supply stashed away. Things I had never seen before all kind of tins, all sorts of different drinks and in mass. In the attic room was all kinds of the best soap and other goodies. I did not say a word to anyone as the widow of the former owner was the only other one who had a key to the room.

In the future I helped myself from these stores to whatever we needed at home or whatever I needed for trading. I don't know if the owner's wife ever noticed her stores going down and if she did she did not let on. She could not have said anything anyway. They were her undeclared goods and she was not supposed to hoard them. I traded such things as butter, bacon, eggs and wurst from the farmers and took everything home. Sunday mornings I went around to villages to my contacts and loaded up. On the way home I avoided one village, that was the one which had a policeman. If he had seen me he would have to stop me because nobody could guess how I was loaded down on the bicycle. I always made it home all right as Hamstern (Hording) as it was called was strictly forbidden. Penalties were very harsh. I liked this time at the store. At Christmas we always got plenty of presents. In general it was considered good working for Herr Rakow.

At home my father was working as a bricklayer again but no

local work so he was posted in Posen in Poland. He wrote home that there were lots of things which were not available at our place or only on coupons. One day mother and I took a train to Posen. We stood with friends and I rode on the streetcars all day and looked at the big city. To the conductor I only said straight ahead and I traveled from end to end for 10 pfennig. All Germans had to travel in the first car. All poles in the trailing cars were marked poles only. It was a yellow patch with a purple P. In Posen I heard about bunkers on the outskirts of town from the First World War. I looked all these over good - some were 10 to 20 Meters in the earth with lots of concrete. Posen at one time was a citadel town that's why all the fortifications. We made 2 trips to Posen and I always came home loaded. Mother bought mostly clothes. In 1940 the Jews were still there and they gave my mother a good deal. When they disappeared in our city in the 1930's I do not remember. I heard the stores changed ownership and on one had been Jacobi I saw a big Star of David on the store front for a while. The other store changed hands so fast no Star of David was on there. This Star of David showed everybody it was a Jewish store and no good German shopped at a Jewish place. Where the owners went to I never heard. It was said that all had a good deal of money. Not all Jews had left. I saw one woman for a long time with the Star of David on her dress. She was rather frail looking. My mother knew her habits and where she walked. Mother always had a sandwich ready and gave it to her while passing on the walk.

At the store, we had a big parking lot. The Milk truck with 2 trailers came every day from the big baron estates. It had the driver and 2 helpers. They had lots of milk cans to handle every day. The driver was called to the army one day and a Polish P.O.W took over driving. He had been a helper for some time on the tractor. This Pole did exactly the same work as the original driver had been doing, but he had to wear the Yellow badge of the poles on his coat. He drank just as hard as the original driver but he was not welcome. All poles were not allowed to come to a bar and order a drink. They were not allowed to drink with Germans if the Guesthouse had only one room meaning that no poles could mix with Germans in one room. Our bar had 3 rooms. The pole never looked for trouble. He knew he was not allowed in the main room and just waited his turn in the 2nd room, not that this was any different. At times they did get served later but that could not be helped. You could not serve all at once. If he had come in the main room he would have been welcome as everyone knew him as a good worker and he could speak German. The local express forwarder had 2 French prisoners working for him real strong men both had to be back at camp every night. At times I got them drunk when they had delivered coal. I don't think they ever complained of bad treatment. In the end or near the end both escaped. There was not much work for them anyway we never heard if they ever made it back to France.

One day in 1943 I saw 2 English prisoners in the city. Usually the English were not made to work as they were still at war with Germany. I really looked their uniforms over as they were different from the Polish and French. What I realised 3 years later was that I had the same uniform as a prisoner in England. I often remember the day I looked at the first Englishman in their uniform, even though the war with Russia was on I had not seen any Russian prisoners yet.

In the beginning of May 1944 I was in Berlin. The capital of Germany looked like a pile of rubble to me. There was not one street which was not bombed from end to end. I found myself near a big church where I saw a lot of Wehrmacht staff cars.

About 15 cars with little flags displayed. I heard there was a funeral service for a former high ranking officer. It could have been a General. Up to this day I have not been able to find out who this could have been in the beginning of May. The church service was not too long. As I looked on, officers of all ranks came out of the church they went into the cars and sped away to the cemetery. As I was near a street intersection I remember quite clearly a colonel with the oak leaves to the knights cross was standing on the running board of his car and motioning with his right arm up and down to the cars to drive faster. Such was a funeral in Berlin in 1944, because whoever this was had to be buried before the American flying Fortress came over again to disturb the rubble. To me it looked like a funeral in panic attended by Wehrmacht officer's who happened to be home from the front. Berlin was not a good place to be. The Allies at this time were already bombing the Fatherland at will. One City after the other was reduced to rubble.

Chapter Eight: Called Up for the R.A.D.

Time went fast for me during these years as I had always had lots to do. Then one day I came home and here was that letter again, the call up for the Reichsarbeitdienst (R.A.D.). This was the last week in May 1944. I had a few days off and the letter said I had to report on the 6th of June 1944 to the labor camp about 120 KM from home. Little did I know that this date 6th of June was to become a famous date in history. By the morning of the 6th I had everything in order in the store. I had more or less cleaned everything out. In the HJ I had turned everything over so I was free to start on a new venture at 17 years of age. I left on the morning of the 6th of June with the information that the long expected invasion in the west had finally begun. Lots of people considered this to be a blessing and all hoped the war would be over soon. It was not to be. We didn't have much trouble with enemy planes in Pomerania. In our area there was nothing to bomb and we were the furthest from England. We had heard a few bombs that was about all. In April 1942 or 43 to be exact it was on Hitler's birthday. We heard an alarm early in the night. Everybody expected Berlin to be bombed here the big parades took place in earlier years. By this time, the bombers came by the hundreds at night.

They sure came this night. It was not Berlin where all the flack had been concentrated in expectation of an attack. The bombers came to Stettin. This was a really big attack as Stettin was 10 times smaller than Berlin and it just about leveled the city. I had seen Stettin on my way back from Peenemunde. It was just nice. We were a good 100KM in a straight line from Stettin and we could hear the noise of the bombing as a distant rumble and we saw the glow in the sky from a 100 KM away from the fires. Stettin burned for over a week. My tante (aunt) Anna who had lived there came back to us after this. Later we heard the Catholic priest had a radio transmitter and they had radioed to England a message which said Grosmutter vereist kinder aleine zuhause (Grandmother on a trip children alone at home). Grandmother meant the heavy Flack like the 88, which had gone on a trip to Berlin. Children were the light Flak like 3.7 alone at home meant with fighter protection. So when the bombers came that night they unloaded with no difficulty whatsoever on the factories big plants. Plants for gasoline production were not bombed this night. In Stettin there was a sugar factory and the sugar burned for weeks. An old part of the town was surrounded by a wall and after the bombing it was not possible to get through the rubble to whatever was in there. Only the dead were left. Nobody went in there anymore for fear of the plague or the likes. How true the message of the Catholic priest was nobody ever found out. The church was just not the same anymore after that.

My mother listened to Radio London at 12 noon because it broadcast in German and she had heard all kinds of things from there. Sometimes she talked about it after the heavy bombing of Hamburg in 1943. She had heard that England had stated that one German city after the other will we reduce to rubble. These were words truly spoken. It happened exactly as said. One night we had an alarm and one bomb dropped the next morning. People were busy looking for leaflets because there were more leaflet dropping than bombing that night. I went looking for leaflet too. Not far from home I saw paper in a tree this I figured could only be a leaflet. I got the paper down somehow and it was a leaflet that said that Hitler had sacrificed 4 million Germans on the Eastern front. What a coincidence 10 years earlier I had read a communist leaflet in this same area dropped from Junkers. The headline gave many people something to think about. We counted the fallen and reported missing in one village and came up with a count of 12 so we could easily add this up to other places and the 4 million figure did not seem so far out of place. Even so we did not believe it.

As mentioned before, the years 1940 and 1941 were good. Then one morning in 1941 we heard to our surprise that German troops had started to attack soviet Russia. How the troops had been shifted from the west to the east was a puzzle to us as we had not seen transport trains going behind our house. The news of the attack in Russia shocked everybody. Even we as children had learned in history lessons that Germany should never fight a 2 front war. This was to be avoided and everybody

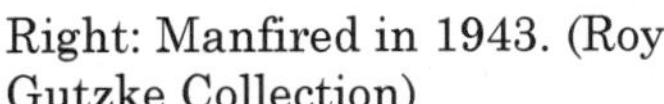

Right: Manfired in 1943. (Roy Gutzke Collection)

remembered the northern lights that they had seen over the area in 1939. After a few months with war with Russia more solders had fallen than in Poland and France combined. Then the terrible cold weather of 1941 to 1942 set in and everything in Germany was mobilized to collect clothing for the front. It was a big effort and helped to prevent a disaster in Russia. This country was so big and after 1942 no maps in Germany were shown which showed Russia past the Ural Mountains. Up to the Urals is only a little part of Russia. The soldiers which came home from Russia spoke of the primitive Russian people and the bravery they defended their homeland with. Some said only a few Russians had rifles and the bodies piled up high but they always kept coming.

In 1943 the man from the milk truck came home from the Russia Front. He of course stopped in our bar. I had never seen such a change in a man after 2 months of nonstop fighting in Russia. He had aged years in a way that he was a broken man even though he was no older than 30. He had been in fighting in the Wolchow front. He did not look forward to the day he had to go back. All soldiers had lice now and their uniforms did not look good anymore. It went downhill slowly for sure. In 1942 the summer was another big effort. We were shown the Tiger tank on the newsreel and it was said the German soldier has the best. No matter what was said, people did not like it. In the fall everyone followed the push to Stalingrad. The papers published what Stalin had said “die stadt die meinen namen traegt darf nicht in des feindes hand fallen”(The city that carries my name shall not fall to the enemy). As the winter went on news of Stalingrad became more desperate. After a while it was clear what was going to happen as people could see the actual front line on the map and the distance to Stalingrad. Then on the morning of January 3 – 1943 we heard the news that the 6th army had surrendered. It was exactly 10 years and one day after Hitler took over Germany. The disaster that everyone knew about was played down by the Nazi propaganda.

They announced our grave losses as 3 Romanian divisions, one other division and one German Flak division. I thought that this was not much. On the day of Stalingrad surrender, people had the same feeling as 10 years earlier when Hitler took over. A feeling of despair and loss with no direction to go. It felt like someone had gone over the country with a sickle and mowed everything down. After this the losses in our village were higher and every day you heard of somebody else. It never ended. I always said later that the 3rd Reich under Hitler lasted exactly 10 years and one day. Many will consider this to be true.

With all this behind me over the years I looked forward to the labor service. It had been reduced to a 3 month term. The invasion had started, but it was a long way off from our area. For a while before the invasion people always said, "let them come we will throw them back the same as a few years earlier at Dieppe". Then gradually things changed because they came and in time it was clear that it would be a success and that they won't be thrown back.

Sometime in the afternoon on the 6th I arrived at this R.A.D. Camp. It had wooden barracks, with a center square for a parade ground. One side was another open space, this was used for exercises and some sport. Rise was 7am with an hour to get ready. During the morning hours it was mostly sport and some exercise. At noon there was one hour break. After that, some lectures or work with the spade. We learned how to handle all kinds of tools the right way. We learned that a spade was used to move small amounts of earth a short way, this was true as long as we were at camp. Later we had to move big amounts of earth a short way.

At about the 3rd week I was picked with 3 others for guard duty. This was considered an honor to have the first guard. Everything went well. Spade exercises were just perfect and we were on guard. The same day we were visited by a higher R.A.D. leader. He apparently had brought new instructions as our foreman was talking of going to the rifle range for a day. This was true. Everybody fired 3 rounds from a .98 carbine. For many, it was the first time they had fired a .98 carbine. Some did not hit anything. I myself did well the first round. I scored a 12. Then everybody had to take the helmet off, Next round was an 11. Next a 12. With this I shared 35 score with only one other in another group. The reward was a half day off duty.

All the time we had kept an ear open for news from the invasion. There wasn't always much about the sources at the perimeter. We heard that some unidentified bombs had exploded in London. Later fuzzy pictures were shown in the paper and on these pictures I recognized the shape of the things I had seen in Peenemunde 2 years ago. Now the funny noise we had heard these things made sense. It was a rocket engine of course I could only say I had seen them but that was all I knew about them.

During the 3rd week we started training like an Army. Attack and camouflage. We also received more clothes and a Bag to carry this stuff in. This was all done within 1 day. The military training continued for about 2 more days and then we received Belgian 7 m/m carbines. Later when I was with the Waffen SS I found that the training material we had in the R.A.D. was left over from the first war. In other words it was good for nothing. On the next day after receiving the rifles we marched to the railway station 12km away, boarded a train and left towards the east. The distance we traveled was not that far. In normal times 5 hour by train it took us 2 1/2 days. We had been in camp approximately 4 weeks. By the time we left Danzig station I had an idea where we were going to go, I had heard all the station names from my mother who had traveled here in 1939. It happened to be the same line just a difference of 5 years. We came through such places as Treuburg – Goldap in East Prussia. In Treuburg not far from the station was some kind of an open place that was partly parkland. There was a monument with an inscription, "Herr Gott Erhore unser Flehen Lass Wieder Ein Einiges Deutschland Erstehen (Lord God Hear Our Begging Let There Be a United Germany Again)".

People who had inscribed this surely had no idea what was ahead for Germany and at that time this referred to the Polish Corridor which cut East Prussia off from the rest of Germany. As we traveled through the Missourian Lake District we saw lots of women working in the fields. This we relished because it was the area where Hindenburg had defeated the Russian army in the war 1914-18. Closer to the old German-Polish border we noticed that earth fortifications were thrown up. All the labor was done mostly by women. In the morning of the 3rd day we crossed the border into Poland. There was no need to mention at this border was visible within 100 meters. On one side the houses in Germany all brick and nice red shingles with a garden. Across the border in Poland wooden houses and no garden so just by looking and comparing the houses you could tell the border. The railway line was quite heavily traveled there were other transports. ammunition trains. Also Red Cross trains. On our first stop in Poland, which was not far in, we were handed 100 rounds of ammunition. We were also told to load. All at once standing on a siding we had entered partisan country. After a stop and go period we stopped again and heard that the train ahead of us had been shot at only 1 km ahead.

As the train had only the usual guard we had got word for assistance. The engine and one car left at once with 40 men. As soon as they arrived at the other train they were involved in a fire fight with small arms. It was only a handful of partisans but in the forest they were hidden and they tied the line up for hours. The partisans lost with one killed. We did not know if we had any losses. After this was cleared up we were on our way again. It was slow progress. Early in the afternoon we were stopped. We seemed to be near some soldiers near a clearing. It was very confusing as we were supposed to go further on. This clearing was not big, all-around was high pine forest. Our leaders started to run around quite uneasy about something they said they had heard from the soldiers that the Russians were just ahead. The forest was unnaturally quiet. I had been in the bush at home for years. In all the time I had not experienced such an eerie feeling in a forest. Shortly afterward we heard that the front line was just ahead of us and if we had continued to our destination, we would have been blown off the tracks. We asked our troop commander how long we would be able to holdout the Russians. He did not answer. It was not a question of stopping as our right flank was already overrun and on the left was a swamp. (I did not know this at this time but this was as far East as I would ever go into Russia)

One Railway car was open and we received bicycles. All the names and numbers were written down. Things had to be in order even so the Russian soldiers were properly watching us, We heard them singing at times as we had all this done then all of a sudden we left in a hurry. The train had already gone so we biked our way back. Even so I did not fire a shot. I would say my first acquaintance with the front line was one of retreat; 2km back on the road we biked on we met a Tiger tank unit they were surprised to see us. Only their experience as old soldiers saved our unit. Our R.A.D. uniforms looked very much like the Russian. I sure looked the Tiger tank over. The wide tracks and the roar of the engine surely impressed me. When we left the tank unit their commander had advised us on how to travel. We sent 3 bikers ahead and told the artillery ahead that we were not Russians. The artillery was about another 3km back where we had been with the train which was no man's land. We biked for about 2 more km. The first farm we came to was deserted and we took it over, we bedded down in the barn and we were here for 2 weeks. The next morning, we had our spades returned, biked into the field for about 2km and here we started to dig a Schutzengraben (Rifleman's trench)

This was about the middle of July. Our leaders or commanders had absolutely no experience in the field. I would say they learned this fast. In the R.A.D everything you did had to be perfect. The trench had to be 1.20 or 4 feet deep 80cm nearly 3 feet wide at the top 1 1/2 foot or 40 cm wide and at the bottom the wall in front 1.20 meter or 4 feet wide and rising to the height of the blade from the spade. Every 8 meters the trench zigged and zagged. As measure was used, everyone was shown how to use the spade in one section only and that was it. In a way we were lucky it was sandy soil that was easy to shovel. The average was about 16 meter of trench in 8 hours. You worked hard to do this and besides in July the sun was beating down on you and the one litre of brewed coffee was soon drunk. One litre was supposed to last for the day. Under normal conditions it probably would have been enough. Not when you shovel under a blazing sun. We were only 3km at the most back of the front line.

On the 3rd day, fighting along the line was very heavy. In the morning the Russian plane I.L.62 or the butchers, nicknamed slaughterers, were flying along the front with everything ablaze. The Russian called these planes Stormovicks. The flack was firing like mad as the planes were not very high. No plane was downed, as we learned later they had armor plating on the bottom. While this was going on, all of a sudden we were yelled at by our commanders to dig yourself a foxhole. We realized we were in the open.

They did not have to tell us again. The first thing we did was dig a foxhole for ourselves and then continue with the trench. Every so often the commander walked up and down that everything was nice and neat. It had to be. Food for the first day was adequate. We had a hot meal in the evening. Something to drink was another problem. Thirst is by far worse than hunger and we were thirsty. By 11 am everybody was out of his liter of coffee. There was a lake nearby but with all the mosquitoes around (we did not dare drink from the water). One day one of the men was digging in a low spot to his surprise he saw that water collected in one hole in the bottom of the trench. This of course was good water. It did not take long and everybody was wise to it. Everyone soon had his own seep hole. Once you started drinking from it you just got thirstier. It was just terrible after about 3 to 4 days. Some of us reported sick. A bit of a fever. This sickness was soon connected with the water. After that no more extra waterhole. I kept one though. Whenever the Sergeant came near I threw a few spades of sand in the hole and that filled it in. After he had gone I opened it again. One day I could not stand it any longer. I had not been sick and my thirst was just unbearable. I went to the next swamp and I just drank. I went back twice more. Two days later I was sick with the fever. Everybody had been sick by now and we finally had a water station during the day. This was just boiled water.

It helped, but once you had the fever it did not make any difference you were able to drink all the seeping water you liked. After about 10 days we moved it a bit further up the line. Here we quarried in the park of an estate in tents. 4 men to a tent dug into the ground 50cm. From here we traveled back everyday by bike to the area. We had to dig in. At times we built bunkers or in placements for machine guns, strung barbed wire and put anti personal mines in. One day we had a detail in the forest, which before was all open field. In this forest near the water where we had to dig the mosquitoes came just like dive bombers several of them were on you all the time. Most of us lasted one day in the forest. We had no repellant no netting. It was pure hell. I wasn't there the next day. I was a day and night guard at the camp. Guard duty was nothing compared to the mosquito forest. Not much was going on during the day on guard. At night the first watch 8 to 10pm was all right. After 10pm usually every night the U.V.D came, which was a one engine plane with the motor sounding as if he was going to crash any moment. This plane flew a few km behind the front line or near it up and down for hours. Sometimes he came back in the morning hours. He never showed up in daylight. He was never shot at as he was just a big nuisance. It was a Russian tactic to keep everyone awake. Some said he carried no bombs just scrap metal which he threw overboard as he saw fit. It was dangerous too. For morale the plane was absolutely perfect. He did not let you sleep. His engine always on the verge of stalling and you could not see him. You knew he was only a few hundred meters up you were just helpless. Everybody hated the U.V.D. This was not just one plane. Most troops in the east reported the U.V.D in all sectors. On another night we were on guard duty again and to a 17 year old a bush in the field became a monster after a while. This one night it did not take long to start shooting. As soon as I heard the first shot I went down and just fired away. I saw nothing. The one with me was behind me. I yelled to him to shoot to the other side as I did not want to be shot by him. I know I fired at nothing so did he. Our Group leaders came rushing out to see what was going on. He had lots of trouble getting us to stop. The next day we had an ammunition count and 30 men had fired nearly 1000 rounds for nothing. The one who started to shoot said he had seen someone ahead of him. That was it we were detailed for another night guard duty. This suited me fine it was better than going back to the mosquitoes

During the time we were in the forest. One man had forgotten something on his way home. He went back by himself. We were just green and inexperienced. As he was alone looking for the lost article he was shot at. What saved him was the trench. He reported the shooting and next day we searched the forest. What we found was really quite something. A good way in we came to trees with the bark removed all around for about 6 feet (2 meters). There was quite a number of trees. We went in deeper and came upon a group of people living in lean-tos built from the bark of the trees we had seen stripped, there were some men, women and children about 30 people as we heard hiding from everybody; the Germans and the Russians and had not shot at our men last night. We left them alone and never even searched the place. We were green. The day after our group leader said we should go and shoot the bunch of them, but the next one up would not give the okay. He just said go and have another look. By the time we did this, the people had left.

On the next day we were well organized - by now we had a horse and wagon. This was good for living off the land. Around 10 am our group leader looked us over and everybody had to tell him how they had done at the rifle range at home. He knew me so I was picked plus 4 others for the driver with the horse and wagon. What had happened was the heavy fighting had always been by a small town waiting to be captured by the Russians. Word had go out by about 4pm. It would be cleared so whoever wanted something, just anything, could make his way in and carry away whatever he wanted. The wagon had already left and we were not told were we had to go or what we had to do. All of us went into the town. This was a typical Polish town with low houses in an open plan. You could see people coming for miles as the dust this time of year just long in the air. It made no difference to us. One car of another unit had joined us to make dust and gave our position away. Close to town our leader told us what he wanted us to do. We were scared. The wagon went to the Market Square and in one house there was wallpaper. The leader wanted wallpaper so we risked our lives for his stupid wallpaper, in the market there was also a Volkswagen amphibious Schwimwagen. This was the first one I had seen. The driver was loading something and he wanted to leave. He just came running back jumped in his Volkswagen and was gone. He had seen the Russians around the corner. He wasted no time and got out of there. This town, Augustowo, was the last the Russians captured for the next 5 months as the front line had come to a standstill.

During this time we got a Newspaper called the Landser or the "Solder" one day I read Gross Deutschland nahm Sudeten. Now this Sudeten was a place of about 5,000. A typical Polish Russian settlement as the border around here had changed at times in favor of Poland. What was strange about this notice was that it took a crack division like the Grossdeutschland (Great Germany) to clear a place like Sudeten of the Red army. Here the Russians did not choose to fight here because they had come a long way in their last offensive and they were not prepared for great pressure on a particular point. It was better to give it up. For the Grossdeutschland division it was hailed as a great victory.

In the daytime we still saw planes flying around. Along the front the flak as usual was heavy but the line held. One day we were home in our quarters cleaning our gear. In the morning a war correspondent visited us with a movie camera. He had a helper with him. As he saw us cleaning our gear, he did not think it was worth taking a shot. He wanted action. We warned him not to go another 3km to the line, but he did not listen. He was back in the afternoon and he was happy to take our pictures, as he considered himself lucky to be alive. News was not reaching us fast. We heard of the attempt on Hitler's life on the 20th of July. Three or 4 days later then only a little news but only for about 2 days and that was it. We were glad that the overthrow attempt had failed.

We had no desire to meet the Russians up close. The weeks went fast during the day. We swam in the river in the evenings. No exercise or other nonsense. Food all the while was not too plentiful. By now in August of 1944 some fruits had started to ripen. Near our camp there was a big tomato field. It was strictly forbidden to go there and take tomatoes. We could see them from the road on the way home. My hunger was worse than all the verboten. I went in at night and the next day I had 90 tomato's. I eat them all on the same day. After that nothing stopped me anymore.

I went out in the evening to the local farms and helped myself. One time I saw a tree near a farmhouse with good apples, I called a friend of mine that we would go get some. He came along and near the tree we found a 15 gallon milk can. It was full with peas. We picked it up and started to carry it off. At this time the farmer came out. My friend was scared so he dropped his side and took off. It was too much for me to carry so I left it. I had the rifle with me and the farmer had nothing. After that I always went alone. It worked better and I kept what I had. It was to an advantage if you had grown up on a farm in the country you know more tricks. Besides one hot meal a day we got 2 packages of Knakebrot. This was some kind of hard biscuit, similar to Melba toast, that after 3 days all your gums were cut up and you could not eat anything. Besides I did not like it. This Knakebrot was standard food out on the Eastern front. Goebbels the minister of propaganda said at home, "We succeed to deliver one wagon of knakebrot to the eastern front". This was an admittance that the partisans were quite successful in disrupting rail supplies. One wagon for the whole eastern front showed he was at his best. Really sarcastic jokes.

When Cologne was bombed it was said the Reichminister of Cologne phoned and said, "Goring Her ist Cologne rest" Goring said yes I hear you Cologne West, "No not Cologne West Cologne rest", Goring hung up. Things like that made the rounds by now. In the first week of September we knew our time of 3 months was about up. We were eagerly waiting to get out of here. The front line was getting hot. For 2 days we were pulled away from trench digging and went up to reinforce the infantry in Warsaw where there was some kind of uprising. We did not hear much of it. Only that some troops had left for Warsaw. We later found out this was the Warsaw Ghetto uprising.

On one day in the first week in September we biked to a railway in Germany. From here we left for an R.A.D camp in Germany, but not the one we had been to before. All our civilian clothes had been shipped here. It took us again 2 days to reach the camp and soon as we were home so to speak. All our troop leaders got their big mouths back. It was useless though and the next day we got our civilian clothes and had the last laugh. On the afternoon before we left, a rumor got around the camp that there would be a meeting in the canteen in the evening, as some call up papers had arrived from the army.

On the night of the meeting everybody was hoping it would not be them. I did not have to wait long my name was about 5th. This was the 8th of Sept. We left camp on the 9th and my papers said to report to the 3rd Waffen SS Flak regiment in Munchen on the 10th of September. From the beginning I had no intention of being there on the 10th. I had my nose full so to speak and needed a rest anyway. I went home first and looked around. What I did learn in the R.A.D that was how to pick potatoes real fast. For a while I always got up from the table hungry and I could not figure why as there were enough potatoes. Just not got enough peeled. Next day I watched the city kids, who always had to fight for potatoes at home, I soon saw what I did wrong and kept peeling enough for myself. When I had one peel I dropped it nicely on the table from the knife. The others did not bother to drop every peel. They just piled it up against the knife and it went real fast. Next time I had enough potatoes.

I had written home twice from Poland and mother expected me about the 8th of September. I arrived at the station in the evening and walked home in the dark. It was just as well that it was dark. Next day I walked through the village and what I saw I did not like at all. It had changed. But as long as I had been there I had seen all the changes and did not notice it much. After an absence of 3 months and returning in the fall things did not look good. The war was now 5 years in and time began to show that fences were down or gone altogether and the street was in need of repair. Homes needed painting and repair. I found the picture rather depressing. In the afternoon I visited the store in town. There were no men folk there anymore. What little bit there was to sell was easily done by the girls. The store closed later on as it was just sold out and only some stores received supplies for ration cards. Gobbles had declared the total war and whatever was not necessary was done away with. The Nazis were on their last breath. After the attempt on Hitler it was only brute force that held the country up. In the East, nobody wanted to surrender anyway. In the west the Allies had made big gains, which more or less I had not heard. The Allied Air Force was flying at will day and night over Germany.

After one big raid on Hamburg my mother took one woman in who's home had been bombed out. More bombed out people had been quartered in the village. One family had friends in Berlin. They were here too. They had a son some years younger than I was. He had spent every summer in the village and I played with him, then in 1941 in the summer he showed me a few splinters from bombs which he had found in Berlin. That was a big thing to have a splinter. A few years later, I wished I had never seen these things, as I had bombs dropped on myself by now. The next day at home I went to the local Military office and told them that I was in possession of my call up papers but they had come with today's mail and it said I was supposed to be in Munich by today. He could see that was impossible. He said I should have had the postman's mark when delivered. I told him that I did not get this kind of mail every day. I had no idea what was in it and I had just returned the night before from the R.A.D. then he mumbled something like 3 day home visit and I think he stamped it. I was in no hurry to leave for Munich, I was home for another day and then I took the train to Munich before I did this. I climbed my favorite tree in the village, an Oak tree and carved my initials in there real deep. I had a sense that I would not be back to this place. This was in 1944. Now in 1977 I had not been back yet in 33 years. I did not say much to my mother as I left on September 11 1944 as she had been through this quite often with my father. We had found it better to just go and don't look back. The local Railway station was good that way. As soon the train moved it went into a curve and one was out of sight. I went to the station myself. The trains were just full for connections one had to wait at a time for hours. I checked twice on the train and it was 1000km kilometer from home to Munich so 2 checks was not bad. The patrol saw that I was late reporting but what could they do. I was heading in the right direction and no train was on time, if it ran at all. The cities I came through looked pretty grim. The stations all partly bombed, everything overcrowded and dirty I had a long stopover in Berlin. Here I walked around a while and what a change from last time I had been here in the spring of 1944. It was plain to see the bombers had been here often and had done a good job.

Left: Manfred in 1944. (Roy Gutzke Collection)

Chapter Nine: Reporting for Duty

The trains I was on were not attacked and I made it to Munich on the 13th in the morning. The first thing I did at the station was to have a beer. I had heard so much talk of Munich beer and the stein it was served in. I just had to have one. Money was no problem with me as in the labor service we were paid 25 penning a day. Plus 3 mark a day for front line duty. So I had been on the front for 35 days it had added up. Over 100 marks was quite a bit of money. As a soldier I only got one mark a day for the next months, so all the money from the R.A.D came in really handy. After the beer I asked for the direction to the Freimann barracks. What a lot of trouble I had. I came from Pomerania and the Bavarian people speak a dialect I just could not understand. I finally found someone who was going partly to Freimann and I traveled with him on a streetcar and bus. I had to walk a while to the Barracks but what I saw I liked in a way as I came near. I could read in big letters over the gate SS Stadarte Grossdeutschland. I reported to the guardhouse and was escorted to the office by an SS man. In the office they checked my papers asked me how come I was 3 days late. I just said on the 10th of the month I was still looking at the Russians so nothing further was said. They knew things were not normal anymore. So I started my time in the Waffen SS. I wore a hat with a skull figure in front which I had seen 3 ½ years earlier by my boss at home.

One thing was for sure, once you walked through that gate you had a feeling of something big. All the atmosphere was good. It was just a man's world. All the things I had seen in the H.J and labor service were kids' stuff. All that was left behind and once inside the gate, it was just so much different. The registration and detaining did not take long. The barracks were built in an open square 5 floors high and on the open side there was a sport hall. The office tower had 12 floors. At the gate on the back of one side was the officers' quarters and the other side was the officers mess and some stables for horses. Here were a few horses for some of the officers, on the back of the buildings was a gate in the surrounding fence. This gate was what we used most. Near this exit were 3 wooden barracks all enclosed in barbed wire. For a few days we did not ask what this was all about. We saw some men in striped suits in there all the time. All were bald and some looked kind of rundown. After a while we heard the 3 barracks were a Concentration camp. It was also a compound for SS men under arrest who had not been sentenced. At the time I

didn't think they had it that bad as we were punished a lot harder and longer. Most of the time they were digging in some big hole near the gate. We never heard how they were treated otherwise. Once we had lunch at 12 noon. We were hardly bothered after 12 o'clock that day. We watched the men in the striped suits and we could tell they were hungry.

The guard with them was just plain mean because he exercised them for about 15 minutes. After I had finished in the office another SS man showed me where I had to bunk down and informed me which group I would belong to. I had just looked around and the men I was to join came in for lunch. They were a real noisy bunch and just plain exhausted and this by 12 noon. I had never seen men so finished by noon and did not think it was true what I saw. They stormed in the room and their gear flew every which way. Helmets gasmasks rifles everything was just

Above and opposite page: postwar photographs of the barracks at Stadarte Grossdeutschland. (Roy Gutzke Collection)

dropped. It was good that no N.C.O. bothered us during this time. I did not go on duty in the afternoon. I went to the stores to get all the uniform articles then back to the office for the S.S. SOLDBUCH. This book you had to carry all the time when you were in uniform. So far everything went well. I had more gear than I cared for and everything was listed. Two weeks later I found out I was short the ammunition pouches. When the gang came back in the evening they looked the same as at noon and they did not know if they had to go out again for night training. I cared very little my mind was made up. I received my uniform in a German SS barracks. I did not know that I would finally have to discard it 1 ½ years later. It would be in England under the watchful eyes of a Tommy. I would say by this time I was glad to be rid of it. It hadn't seen a cleaning in 1 1/2 years.

The next morning rise was at 6 am. There was still a bugler on the barrack square. From 6 to 7 am. You just about fell over yourself. Everything went full blast on the double all the time. I had 2 days or mornings of this mad nonsense in the morning. The 3rd day at noon, the Sgt Major asked if everyone had been a batman to someone before. This could only mean that an officer in the company needed one. I had this figured out real fast and stepped forward. I was only asked when and for who. I said for a staff Stg. This was good enough. I became PUTZER for the lieutenant in our Battery. This suited me fine. The mad rush in the morning was solved. If anybody wanted anything of me, I just said sorry I have to see the lieutenant. This solved everything for me all the time. A cozy job. I had to do regular duty but nothing else, like sweeping up the room or getting coffee, none of that. The lieutenant was a good man, about 28 years old and well educated. He went on orientation for a week and he gave me all his ration cards for the officer's mess and I made good use of that. Their food was not far different from ours. In all it was a good gesture. Most of the time it said on the duty roster: "Duty by H.D.V. 131 HEERESDIENST VORSCHRFEFT. 131". This meant field exercise. We marched out the back gate and here was a very large open area just a man-made hill from the hole the striped suits had excavated.

This open area was at least 2 square Kilometers. On the end of it was forest. To the left a little bush on a hill which was called the HASENBERG. As soon as we were out the gate we were on our storm march this meant up and down till we came to the forest on the far end. After that we just went back. Then we went back again. If that was not enough a run was always good. After that we were allowed to hop along like a kangaroo with rifle held up front. Then we were allowed to put the gasmask on as we wanted to run 2 km. By the time it was noon you walked on your heels and the morning coffee boiled in your ass. This was the same in the afternoon. The only difference was, we were with the 88 flak and we were allowed to pull the 71/2 ton gun around for one hour. By 5pm you could sleep standing upright. Several days of this and you were used to it and did not find it so hard anymore. At night you were not left alone. No sooner had you gone to sleep and the whistle blew and it was night training for 3 hours. Night training meant going to the bush and someone would make all kinds of noise's until you could identify what made a certain noise like a spade digging in the ground or our mess tins rattling. Later we really appreciated this training. All the while there was no smoking before noon. You could not have lasted anyway in the afternoon if you did you had no chance. It did not bother me as I did not smoke.

When the field exercises were over for the day it was either night training or political lectures in the evening. When that was not enough the bombers came over and kept you up. If they were good they would stay over 3 hours during the night then we got up one hour later in the morning. It was not ideal, but there was a war on. While in the labor service work was 8 hours a day here it was 24 hours a day. On about the 6th day the routine had changed for no reason. Then we heard that we would be sworn in that day. It was traditional to have no duty on this day. By noon we were all lined up in the square and it was the swearing in ceremony. It did not take long and afterwards we were marched out to Munich to visit the house of German art. Here we were let loose and told to be back by 10pm. Everything went well. Nobody was late and the house of art was well worth seeing. It was all covered with nets as camouflage.

Two days later we had to go to the office tower one morning. The medical department was here and everybody had some blood taken. Then you were tattooed on your left arm. After this you could always be identified as a genuine SS man. You also had your blood group tattooed, it was all quite painless.

We were always able to tell it was a Sunday. The day before we had battery exercises and instead of the N.C.O chasing us around on Saturday the Battery officers did the chasing. They were a bit more refined in their know-how and the exhaustion was a bit more complete. After this we always knew it would be Sunday. This meant one hour longer sleep in the morning. Instead of slinging the rifle over our shoulders we donned sport gear and started to run for 10 km. Then we ran another 10km as the N.C.O's were too lazy to start some ball games. I had seen on the newsreel one time how the SS man got his refreshment in sport and play. This had always stuck in my mind. Sunday was not refreshing in sport and in play for us. It was worse than weekdays. It was very hard for some who were not so good in sport. I was about average. I found it hard too, but I could take it. Sunday afternoon after 2pm was free. This happened twice to us. After the 2nd Sunday things really got hairy. Munich was bombed at least once a week the police were overloaded with work. The 3rd Saturday at noon we were ordered to dress up in our A1 uniform to field regulations. While this was going on I saw that all the others put on ammunition pouches. I had a set marked in the Soldbuch as received but I had none. I went down to the store and told the Sergeant. I had probably not received the ammo pouches. Before I could say anymore he asked if I had a sister at home. I said yes, and then he said I had sent them home so that she could have a pair of shoes made out of them. This was the first time I heard that they made good shoes. I told him that this was not so. I just did not get any.

He said okay give something to the Red Cross collection. I put in 20 marks which he claimed was too much. Then he gave me the ammo pouches. No sooner was I back and we were called out at once. We were loaded into a truck and out we went to Munich. Polizeiprosidium. We were driven right into a center yard hidden from the street. Here the license plates were covered and all the instruction we got was when the truck stops the gate will open and you jump off. When you have it sealed NOBODY is to pass you in or out. Everybody received ammunition and had to load the mouser 98. It was just like we were told, the truck stopped and the street was sealed by us in seconds. At first as the people saw what came out of the trucks you could hear there was a near panic, it would have been useless to try anything with us. We had hard duty all week and here was a chance to let off some steam. What was going on here was a black market. Everything what had been plundered by people after or during an air raid was sold here. Most of the time it was traded for something else. One detective was looking for criminals. He was very good as if he could read a man's mind. He gave no quarter to anyone and an arrest was done on the spot.

In this plaza there where several thousand people this afternoon. As the street was sealed I looked around a bit and saw a black man. I believe this was the first black person I had ever seen for real. I started to follow him to see if he was real. By the time I was in the middle of all these black marketers, I did not feel too good and when I spotted the detective with his P38 I joined up with him. With him I searched the lavatory in the middle of the plaza and chased everybody out. By this time some others had joined us and we were told to let no one look over a fence which blocked the view to the search area. One man stood on a bench and I asked him to get down. He must have seen I was just a kid of 17 years old, he made a face and told me to beat it. He never finished whatever he wanted to say. I hit him in his knees with the mouser and he was on the ground before he knew how he got there. At this time I took the safety off and just quickly moved away. Most of these people were foreign workers. It took several hours to check everybody. After dark we returned and 2 of us were detailed to one regular policeman. Our duty was to help him check the bars and parks for strangers without papers. We were in several bars there was not much. Around midnight we went into one was just loaded with people. Soldiers were dancing with girls. Here there was a band playing and dancing just like peace time.

It was hard for us to believe as dancing was forbidden. We had been joined by another patrol at this time and our policeman said he would like to look in here as he himself had never dared to walk in here by himself. It was his beat and he knew what was going on inside. One thing he made us do was to open the collar of our greatcoat so that the SS signs of our uniform were visible and we had to carry the rifle at our hip. It turned out that he was no greenhorn. He had estimated right. As we entered we heard "out with the police". We went into the light. (Entrances were dark for blackout reasons) and the heckling stopped at once. The guests had seen who they had to deal with if they wanted trouble. One soldier came near me. He said something like I should go home and piss in my mother's pot. All he wanted to see though was if the rifle was loaded as any soldier can spot this at a glance. He had seen right. I just had to pull the trigger. Our policeman arrested 2 poles here without papers. On Sunday morning we were returned to our barracks. It had been a good outing for us we did not mind. We were back to the grind on Monday first thing.

About the 5th week one evening, some of my group were told to get up at 4AM next morning and dress in A.I uniform. This was already our best. The evening before this getting up at 4am we had a night exercise as usual. It involved a march of some 15 kilometers. At the halfway mark some others were called and notified to get up a 4am. I had not been told yet. One of them said here it is nearly midnight and we are still out and then have to get up at 4am. He finished saying this and it was just loud enough for our N.C.O. to overhear this but he was not able to identify the speaker. He asked and got no answer. Then he threatened us, but what could he do to us that was worse than what we had been through. He claimed he would split our stinking assholes right up to the neck if we did not give him the name of this man. He never got the name. It is possible he knew all along. He just wanted to see if we would give one of our own up. We did not. If our assholes were to be ripped apart then it would happen to all of us or nobody. Next day this N.C.O told us he was proud of us as we had stuck together and not given anybody up. Then he said if we had, he would have ripped our assholes apart to the neck twice over. He said he was proud of how we

B E S I T Z Z E U G N I S

D E M

SS-Kan. Manfred G u t z k e
(Dienstgrad, Name)

2./SS-Flak Abtl. 4
(Truppenteil, Dienststelle)

ist auf Grund

seiner am 17. 3. 1945 erlittenen
1-maligen Verwundung - xxx xxxxxxxxx

Das

V E R W U N D E T E N A B Z E I C H E N

In "S c h w a r z"

verliehen worden.

Salzwedel, den 28. März 1945

Oberfeldarzt u. Chefarzt
Res.Laz.Salzwedel

Left: Manfred in 1944. (Roy Gutzke Collection) Above: Manfred's orders assigning him to the 4th Flak Battalion. (Roy Gutzke Collection)

held together. This he expected of true SS men. Just a little incident but it taught us a lot. A little after midnight I was informed to get up at 4am. No one knew why yet.

The next morning at 4am everybody was up. After we had dressed we were marched out in the direction of the HASENBERG. This was only a little rise in the flat plain with pine trees on the top. This was all well before sunrise. On the march to the Hasenberg word had leaked out what this was all about. We would witness an execution by sunrise this same day. On the side of the Hasenberg we were lined up in an open square facing the bush. We could see that at the open end was a wooden post in the ground about 4 feet high. We figured somebody would be tied to this post to this spot. Things started to move now as it was not far till daybreak. A man was marched to the open end. An officer came round and said who this man was and confirmed that a court martial had found him guilty of plundering in Munich during an air raid. On top of that, he should have been on duty with his group which was stationed in our barracks. Finding him guilty meant the death penalty. He was tied to the post with just his pants on. From his right, a troop of 10 SS men and an officer came marching in. This was a wet grassy area and the officer of the 10 men tripped in the grass and fell on his nose. We did not laugh. Once in line with the men at the post the commander halted. He turned and the officer called out to the first row to kneel as they had come out in 2 rows of 5 and the first line did so after they had taken their rifles down.

Now the commands came very quick. Aim, FIRE, in between aim and fire was just a fraction of a break. The 10 rifles had all been loaded beforehand and it was said none of the men firing knew if they had a live round in the chamber as the loading was done by someone else and then the rifles were handed out so the loader himself did not know which rifle had a real live round. The moment they pulled the trigger the blindfolded man on the post fell a bit back at first. Then his knees buckled and he just hung on the post with his arms tied to it. I was on his left and I could see the flesh coming out his back when the bullets hit him. He was cut loose and a doctor examined him who he informed our regimental commander that the man was dead. With this we were dismissed and marched home. What a sight to see for a 17 year old. Not too inviting.

The usual drills started at 10 this morning. Near the barracks was our SS 88 flack battery in firing position. This crew was further advanced in training than we were. Whenever there was the sight of allied bombers this battery opened up. We took over this battery 3 weeks later, but before we were called to Munich once more, we spent a week in a maneuver field, then to Munich.

One weekday when there had been a heavy raid on Munich, the police as usual had phoned our barracks for help and we were called in from the training ground. We had to dress real fast, as the truck was already waiting. In the city lots of places were still burning. We were gathered in a church where all the pews had been removed as they were wood and burned easy. It was just the bare floor. We were told the name of the church and the street. Unfortunately I can't remember their names. From here we were split up into groups of 3 and 4 and a policeman showed us once where we had to guard. What I was assigned to guard was a nice villa on a lovely street on the Isar river. All the homes here were big with a large garden. We heard later this was an area where a lot of Nazis had their homes. The guard was changed every 4 hours as this was the best way and we did not have to walk back to the church so often. This is where we had to sleep and got food after the policeman had instructed us.

What was to be done and what did we have to do? We were left alone. What we had to do was to shoot anyone who tried to plunder the place. I walked up to the villa. I could not see much wrong with this. Was I wrong? The front was there and so was a big hole with some bodies. I think there were about 4 bodies including a young girl who was maybe 15 years old. The blast had blown all over the place. It did not interest me much anyway. I sat down in what was left of a room and looked out the opening where a window had been and that was it.

It was October by now and not pleasant outside anymore. I made a round in the garden. When I came back I saw a woman quite close to the house in a bent over position as she was picking something up. I called to her and she hardly paid attention. Next time I called she looked up and saw that she looked down the barrel of my rifle. I had her in the sight when she said something. Moving closer to her I found that I had trouble again understanding her Bavarian language. I made out she was from the house across the street and just wanted to look. I realized she had not understood my Pommeranian accent either. I let her have a look she did and went away without a word never to return to the sight of the half cut up bodies of people she knew was too much for her. The bodies were picked up next day and tagged on a toe if the toe was there. At times parts of different people were thrown in one box. Parts of one of the bodies were mixed with others which I saw in the box. There were 2 men with gloves and it had taken them 2 days to come to the place where I was. The guard duty was for 3 days, not a bad break.

By now we had been trained on the 88. We did quite well and did not pull it around so much anymore. We also went to the range and here we learned to shoot from the hip with the carbine. Also on the run, we only shoot at a target once. At other times it was training for real. No funny stuff. Shoot like you feel from the hip or on the run. We were told to shoot first and you will live longer.

After the rifle training came the machine gun training. I was singled out to be number 1 machine gunner. This was easy I did not have to carry ammunition. This machine gun was called the MG 42, nicknamed `The Hitler saw' by the Russians. This MG42 was so simple, light weight and easy to handle, it was just a good gun. The rate of fire was 900 rounds per minute. What a change to the machine gun I had seen since some years ago in my school this was so much simpler and lovely to fire. I really liked the MG42. After this we were trained on the Panzerfaust 28 meter and the 60 meter this meant a reach of 28 and 60 meters, we fired at a Sherman tank which was on our training ground for firing exercises. The Panzerfaust was easy to aim and really did the job. You could see the head fly through the air and land on the tank for a split second till she had burned through the steel. The Panzerfaust was the first truly disposable weapon. Used once and thrown away. While this was going on with the Panzerfaust we were issued new weapons. This was just to get familiar with them. We were told the name of the weapon was STURMKARABIONER. Did we ever like this Sturmkarabiner. It had a 32 round magazine and fired automatic and single shot. The Sturmkarabiner would be known as the AK47 30 years later. After the war, the Russians army adopted it as their standard issue. I had realized it was good as soon as I had one. So did the Russians.

One day during the early training period in September we were not marched right out one morning. Instead we waited for the Regimental Commander. He arrived and informed us that a large airborne landing had taken place in Holland. He was very correct. He mentioned something like 30,000 parachutists. At the same time he said not to worry as he knew the parachutes had landed on 2 SS divisions. He gave us the names. He also mentioned that some of them had been at the same barracks where we were right now. He said he knew how they would fight and as far as he was concerned this was the second day and the men he had trained were victorious. He was right. This battle would later be known by the Allies, as `A Bridge too Far'. One day we were on a break period around 10 in the morning and we were quite comfortable on the edge of the bush. All of a sudden there was this motion in the sky. We all saw it about the same time. It was a Messershmitt 262 jet plane. It was on a low level flight about 50 meters up. No sound as we saw it first. It had just come over the tree tops. Then when the sound followed, there was not one off us left standing. We were all in Volle Deckung (full cover) in a split second. This was my first introduction to a jet. In low level flight it was an experience of things to come. We had seen some at great heights but nothing like this. The noise of a jet was something strange and scary, absolutely frightening. Later, I experienced low level motor driven plane attacks and it was nothing compared to a jet plane.

By the end of October our training was well advanced. All that was missing was the actual firing of the 88 flak, we did not have to wait long. From one day to the next, we were in a train and on our way to our ubungsplatz (practice grounds) some 100 km away near Angsburg. It was a nice rail trip. I was on the flatcar with the MG42 to guard and shoot at planes in case of attack. I was lucky no planes came. I had not found a hiding place on that flatcar.

We spent 7 days at the training ground. Every morning we marched out singing our way as we went past a P.O.W camp where there were English N.C.O.'s from a Sergeant up. This camp looked pretty crowded at times. The Englishmen looked when we marched past especially the first morning. We were something new to them. We noticed the high barbed wire and the watchtowers. What an irony, here we were marching and singing. We felt good as life on the ubungsplatz was new and good to us. Only 6 months later the ones that were still alive from our company were behind barbed wire. Twenty years later I got talking to a man in Canada who said he had been an Allied P.O.W in Hohenfels. It turned out this was the place where I had marched past. He remembered our company from October 1944. He remembered the singing.

Every day in this place we had different training like bush fighting, pistol shooting, machine gun shooting and 88 firing. It was quite a variety of different weapons to learn. On about the 2nd day we trained in bush fighting. I had one incident the second time I was guard at camp. I heard the firing and saw no reason why I could not shoot too while on guard. I was supposed to be the only one around. I saw a post at a distance at about 89 meters and started shooting at it. I did not aim particularly carefully. Some distance from the post the background was a markup of a Junkers S2 Fuselage that was used by Paratroopers for training. After my third shot I saw men getting out of the Fuselage real fast. Faster than any paratrooper ever did. My bullets had gone right through the wooden post and in the same line of fire the Fuselage. The men which jumped out of it had gone to play cards in there. Now I was not supposed to shoot at wooded post. They were not supposed to play cards. It was a standoff. Nobody reported anything as nobody had been hurt. I gave one man 10 cigarettes in camp and that settled it. I couldn't care less. It was done and forgotten.

One time we had day and night firing at a moving target with the 88. The target was a tank of wood at 500 meters distance pulled by a rope. I think we hit him on the second shot.

At night we had a little fire going near the bush which was cozy. Now we had a guy with us who always put us in a hole. He just did not fit in. We had asked the sergeant to send him to look for firewood. The Sergeant knew what was up and the matter could only be settled by us. We were waiting in the bush for the man. To our surprise he must have sensed that something was up. We never saw him again in SS uniform. As soon as he was out of sight from the fire he was gone. Deserted. Two weeks later back in Munich we saw him in the barracks surrounded with the barbed wire. He had joined the men in the stripped suits. I never found out whatever came of him.

The last day at the field camp I had telephone duty on a road which meant blocking the road as the others were firing with the 88 overhead. It was a cold day. I could see a house not too far away. I went there to warm up and then my friend went. In the end we both went together. It was just plain stupid for us to stand here. As we had stopped one farmer on his cart, he just told us he knew where they were shooting and he went to his field. Later as we came back we phoned central and asked if we could go home to base. They blew their top as they had tried to reach us for a long time to tell us firing was over. We claimed we had been there but no phone rang. He said he was going to report us for leaving the post. He could not prove it. We never heard anymore from him about it though.

Back in Munich our time was not over yet. Something was still to come. The execution of the one man was still quite on ever body's mind and it was with our Regimental Commander. He issued an order as the men had been from his regiment we had to be punished too. He ordered regular duty all day. That meant exercise till you drop. At 9.00pm we were to be ready for a 25km forced march. This meant full gear plus 3 cobblestones wrapped in a blanket and put in your rucksack. Total weight was about 30 pounds. At 9pm, we were ready. To march 25km, for us was a bit over 5 hours. Somehow during the night our leader made a wrong turn at the intersection. As we had marched 30km and our barracks nowhere to be seen he just cut across the field as he knew the direction. This was for about another 4km and it just about killed us. Marching on the street is okay, but the across the field after 30 km it was too much. The last 500 meters within sight of the barracks he yelled gas. We put the mask on. For the last 200 meters he yelled ACHTUNG. This meant we should make the goosestep. It did not work. For sheer meanness he marched us once around the barrack square. This march was about the hardest punishment I had ever experienced. The next day duty started at 8. It was just impossible to move and lots had booked off because their feet were too sore. I had worn no socks but the flannel ranks for my feet. This worked fine. Even so we were told or advised to wear socks. It was about time we got out of this hell hole. Somebody must have heard our cursing.

One day we saw other SS men in our barracks dirty as pigs and nobody bothered them. We had one hair out of place and you ran the square for one hour with full gear. But these men did not salute and did not care one way or the other. We heard the same day they had come up from Hungary where they had fought the southern Russian army to a standstill. This was true and their losses had been heavy. They had managed to save their 88 now they were here for Ersatz or restock of their ranks. This was done from the group ahead of us in training. They joined that division and we moved out to the fire base. This started an all new life again. I had written home quite regularly and mother decided to let my sister Lotte come down and take my good clothes back home. The clothes were usually mailed home but things got lost and a suit with other things was Quite a treasure. Besides it was the only one I had. Everything was obtained through coupons. Coupons did not guarantee you a suit. Sometimes stores had no suits for a long time. It was arranged that Lotte would come to Munich and she had a free pass as she worked for the railway. At first as a station ticket seller, and latter in the freight section in the office. On the day she was to arrive, I had it all arranged with the barracks gate as our company had guard duty. It just so happened we moved out that day. She was a day late with all the bombings on route. Berlin was particularly bad she claimed. It took several hours to get through there.

The next day, a Sunday, I was called to the gate of the fire base and there was my sister. She had been informed by the guards of the barracks where we moved to she walked over and it was quite early in the morning. Now we had to go to Munich for her train. I asked the N.C.O. on duty if I could have the day off he said okay be back at 9. I went back to the gate and said that didn't sound right because 9 was only 20 minutes away. I went back to the N.C.O., he wanted to say 21 hours this was good.

My sister and I talked a lot about home and about how people were very down. There was hardly a family who had not lost somebody or the families were broken up somehow. She also mentioned that the Landwacht was pretty well established by now. The Landwacht started late in 1943 for a while as some prisoners had broken out of camps and the Landwacht were 2 older men from our village patrolling at night. They were armed. People were advised not to leave clothes out at night for drying out overnight as this was the custom in our area. Nothing was ever stolen. In the city the police usually kept an eye on things at night. In our city we still had some policeman from the old school around. They were too old for military service. One was old, but his cheerful disposition made up for it. One day he walked the street and a man passed him. He saw at once that the man had the Nazi party badge on the wrong lapel on his jacket. He did not arrest him right away as he knew he was a phony. There was a law forbidding illegal display of Nazi regalia or badges and medals. He followed the man into a guesthouse and found that the Polish worker there helped prisoners at times. He arrested both. The one with the Nazi badge was an escaped English pilot.

My sister told me they found 2 more in the city station. The switchman was in his house overlooking the yard where a freight train was stopped. One car they had loaded and a tarp over. On the tarp was some water and he noticed that the water stirred every so often. It was all calm. Everybody had been warned about escaped prisoners and you saw one on every corner. Well, the switchman got an officer from the station with some men, there were always some around waiting for transport. The soldiers surrounded the hay car and it only took a bit. Out came 2 men who were English prisoners. Such was the state that even little mistakes gave you away.

I was in Munich with my sister for the day. She took my clothes and I had to leave a bit before the train departed. One time I saw one SS NCO. He was the lowest rank Understormfuhrer, but he had the insignia of a company Major. I was so stunned I did not salute at once. He came back wanted to know where I belonged to. So I just said the SS fire base. He said I should report myself to the NCO on duty at the base on my return. I did not. Next morning all men who had been in Munich had to step forward. I had to as my N.C.O. knew I had been out. I figured this N.C.O. from Munich had phoned and since nothing happened I was looked over. No pass could be found for my absence and no one wanted to take the blame for the N.C.O. So I had not been in Munich. It suited me fine.

At the fire base our clothes were always changed by the stores. One day I must have picked a dirty shirt because I got the itch real bad. I had to go the medic. In his office was a Sergeant Major who I did not know or what he wanted there. Two days later I knew I was on the duty roster for guard duty and the Sergeant Major was always looking for someone for guard duty so I was the one. I have to say from the day I moved into the fire base I did not set foot into a solid house for over 3 years. There was only a little break for 6 weeks outside of that. I would be below ground in a dugout or in a tent for the next 2 years. The guard duty I had to do was at the gate first. This was all right there was no other duty involved with this. 2 hours on, 4 hours off. The next night I had just gone. Guarding this meant regular duty during the day. The 3rd night I was beat. We didn't have a watch so we tried to hear the bell from a church steeple. This did not always work out. After a while I woke my relief and jumped in to bed in full gear before he came out. He never did come out and I fell asleep were I lay. I was shaken awake by the N.C.O. from the guard house. He had made a patrol and saw that there was no guard. It did not take him long to find out who had to be on duty. I expected a hell of a dressing down next morning on roll call. Nothing happened. Next day my name was on the duty roster again. I was on report to the camp commander. Also on report was the worst drill sergeant of the company.

I was called in to see the camp commander. He asked what had happened on my guard. I explained that I had been on guard duty 3 consecutive nights. This was strictly against army regulations. He was very understanding. He asked how old I was I just said 17. He knew he was dealing with kids instead of men as he should have been. His age was about 40. He said he could not let me go free, but he would also not report me as a report would not have looked good for him and I and I would have joined the men in the striped suits. He made this quite clear. I was sentenced to 3 hours punishment duty done over the noon hour drill. The Sergeant with me had to carry it out. So for the next 3 days I reported to him 10 minutes after 12 in full gear with a brick in the rucksack and the drill hour was 50 minutes. Our area was flat there so exercise would have been easy if it wasn't for the bombing raid we had had on our battery a few days before. That day we fired 256 rounds with the 88. We used wet bags to cool the gun barrel. We must have given the planes a hard time. Our fire range officer called though the intercom to all guns. "Bombers on the battery" this meant we all jumped into our fox holes. He had seen the bombs being released from the planes through his rangefinder he also could see that the aim was our battery. We got ploughed over. No injuries thanks to the warning. The guns were dug in and they made it through undamaged from the load of bombs. We found craters all over the place, some quite deep. I had to run or crawl through the craters in the punishment drill. One round for the 88 was 80 marks. There were 8 guns to a battery that fired 2,048 shells so the total cost was 16,384 marks that we shot that day. This day the planes dropped their bombs wildly with no damage.

I made it for the 3 hours. After that I schemed a way out of the mess again. I reported sick with a blister, which had got infected. I was detailed for inside duty for 3 days. Now I had found that the allies came over about 12 noon every day. Our roll call was shifted from the morning to 12 noon as our regimental commander had the bright idea we should get up at 5am because he wanted us to have one hour political lessons from 6 to 7am everyday. He claimed the troops at the front had even less rest then we had.

After the 3 days off sick were over, I did not report fit for duty. I was sick for the next 10 days. My platoon NCO came to me one day and asked if I was really sick. I said sure I was. In any case he said today at 12 noon or the roll call all us sick ones will be asked to show up. I was sick. At 11 45 we heard the Cuckoo on the radio. This was an Air Command Warning Signal at the same time we also got an Alpenrose call this meant one man went to the gun and hooked up the sight and 10 minutes later we had Feuerbereitshaft (Fire Readiness). This was not just a full alarm. The Allies came punctual as clockwork at 12 noon. I was sick, but well enough for gun duty, which I liked. I carried this on for 3 weeks. The Allies worked fine for me. At times we did not fire as it was said German fighters were also up there. These were the jets. Overhead was a stream of vapor trails always 4 in a row and made by 250 planes.

When the planes came over and before we started shooting we used to say shall we say hail Hitler to them up there. Someone else would say H.H is good enough. Or 88 as H is the 8th letter of the alphabet.

Not far from these 350 were another 350 planes. A little while later another 350 planes and this was followed by another 350 planes; one plane for every day of the year. Within an hour we counted 1,000 4 engine planes. What a difference to the 18 I got excited about 5 years earlier. Later we found that the fighters were not German fighters. It was the long range Mustangs escorting the bombers.

One day a new bomb must have been developed by the Allies because these came down like an express train they really roared. In the afternoon we expected the bomber streams back they did not come. The Allies had invented the shuttle service over Sicily to North Africa. Next day they came back from the south this way they faced the flak only on the in flight, as there was no return flight. Things were getting all fully tough for us again. Some men from my platoon were found sleeping during the day under the bed. The N.C.O. found out one day. He went back in the barracks and he heard someone snoring. He did not see anybody in the beds. He found him under one. The N.C.O. just woke him up and the man claimed he had the sleeping sickness, but nothing was said about it, as the N.C.O. should have missed him. They were just as beat as we were. Duty from 5am to 10 pm. Plus night alarm and when we thought we had time to rest it was already 5 am. I had to find a way out of this. I heard that the local INN was looking for help from our battery, which was only 500 meters away. I didn't know how I landed the job but I did. For 3 days I was with an Austrian who could understand the Bavarians. We peeled potatoes, washed the floor and cleaned the yard. Potato peeling was done by machine.

I had never done potatoes by machine. The Austrian had not either. We peeled potatoes till the big ones were small ones all eyes were gone and instead of 3 bags we had 2 bags, which the owner did not like. He really chewed us out. It did not matter to me because I did not understand a word he said. The next day someone else peeled the potatoes and I was back at the battery.

In the last month of 1944, the bombing was just plain terror bombing and was demoralizing the population. Nothing of value was left standing. But the bombs still dropped and moved the rubble over. With the bombing during the harvest the bombers dropped potato beetles, which ruined the crops. They also dropped ration cards. From then on most ration cards were issued weekly. Then they dropped prosperous plastic plates that caught fire when the sun hit them. It did a lot of damage to the wheat fields and they burned before the harvest. If you found a cigarette lighter or a fountain pen you were well advised to leave it alone. The moment you opened them, they blew you to bits. Throughout this area of the terror bombing things got really hard. Then one day one Sergeant approached from our platoon. This was the old drill Sergeant. I figured he was after me again. He asked who was able to fix bicycles as he had to bike to some headquarters every day to get the password for the day because it was not to be given over the phone. The man who had fixed his bike had been transferred and he was looking for a replacement.

I had fixed bikes at home for years. Here was a chance to get off duty again. I said I can fix bikes when I have the repair kit. I knew repair kits were impossible to obtain and the tires were down to nothing. The bike was otherwise sound. Well, I had a little workshop with an oven inside. It had turned cold by now and even the rats had sought shelter in our bunker from the cold. One man did not like rats. One night he left the light on after everybody was in bed, he laid down on the table with the loaded mouser and waited for the rats. This was only a few days after we had watched the execution. I remember I had a dream where I was shot at the end. With this, the man on the table pulled the trigger and blew the rat to bits. I know to this day that my heart skipped a few beats as the shot went off. It was just like an 88 going off near your ear. This was the first and last time he fired the rifle in the confined space.

We had been informed that the V2 started flying. No more was said about it. The whole thing was a secret. It was more or less the same with the Ardennes offensive. (Battle of the Bulge) we were informed about it and told 2 SS groups were spearheading the offensive. It went well for a few days, the rest of the information just petered out.

Then I heard a rumour (The rumour mill always worked faster than the official channels), that we were not pulled out of the Eastern front to be drilled to death here. We were to be transferred to Peenemunde. I knew it was a rocket base for the V.1 and V.2. Within 2 days of this we were on our way and 28 hours later in Peenemunde receiving instructions on the V.2. We had an orientation given by one of the rocket scientist. After an hour and half of him explaining the principals of how the rocket worked he made the mistake of asking for questions. One of the artilleryman put up his hand and asked, "Professor, where is the barrel?" The scientist turned and walked out.

Sometime in November we had a big evening party. I didn't know what it was for. It was said the old Germans had done it and the SS upheld the tradition. I could not care less. This was the time we were all beat and then we had this parade.

By the middle of December I switched from group Dora to group Heinrich because their loader got sick. I did not mind much. Dora was a stationary gun. It had a concrete base. Heinrich was on crossbeams and always ready for transport. I was still fixing the bicycle. Next to the shop was the coal supply. It took me just one hour to loosen some boards and get the coal. Our weekly coal ration was good for 2 days. The Heinrich bunker was above ground and not as warm as the others. With me supplying the coal our bunker was the warmest place in Munich. For wood, we cut trees at the Hasenberg. I would soon do it again.

Christmas 1944 was uneventful, we received lots of cake as the kitchen did its best. Our bunker was decorated from top to bottom in foil. The bombers supplied plenty of it. They dropped tin foil to confuse the radar. It was a good Christmas. We even had one and half days off. Even the bombers left us alone for a day. In all it was a good Christmas compared to a year later. In the first week in January my name was on the duty roster again to report to the office. One older man was with me. We were asked if we wanted to attend an Aircraft Identification Course for 3 weeks. We would have agreed to any course just to get away from here. After Christmas things had picked up again. A few days later we started the course. Every morning we walked to the barrack 2km where we first had been and the course was just like school.

We listened for 8 hours and learned to identify 95 different aircraft from a distance of 3km in 3 seconds, which consisted of 35 German types, 35 English or American and 25 Russian. Here I heard the night planes again which I had already experienced. The other one was the Butcher. While attending this course nobody bothered us.

My friend had not received mail for a long time and he knew the Americans were in his home town. He was from the Saar region.

One day we returned to the base. It was just like a beehive, everybody had to parade his full gear. Rumours went up and down on everything from joining a werewolf unit to going on leave for 18 days. It turned out it was going on leave for 18 Days. Naturally I was not included nor was my friend. We tried higher ups, but nothing worked. We had to finish the course. We were both mad about it, but what else could we do. Sometime later I was glad that I had not been on leave. The SS uniform worked like a red cloth on some people in my village at home. We finished the course and were the official Aircraft Identifiers of the battery. The others came back from leave, but nobody got his gear back. As we had been in the barracks every day we saw another bunch of soldiers dirty from head to foot and not giving a darn about anything. We had seen this before and figured out what was up. These solders belonged to the SS police Division 88 flak unit. They needed reinforcements and it sounded good to us. Two days later we were on a transport with this outfit to the ub-ungsplatz Hohenfels again.

The time on the firebase had made men out of us. Later we found out that it was not as tough in the field unit. We were called comrades and nobody of the N.C.O.s at any time was called Herr or Sir like in the Army. We did not even know the army ranks. In the firebase we had one other hair-raising incident one time during the firing of a grenade that did not go off. We waited the minute as ordered then tried again 3 times. It did not fire. We had a fox hole for such grenades not far from the gun. Everybody except the Gun leader and the K3 leader stand behind the gun leader who opened the breach and the K3 grabbed the grenade and both walked to the fox hole to drop it. On the way to the hole the K3 said, “I can feel through my clothes this thing is getting hot.”

The Gun leader just yelled drop it by this time they were at the hole. Both hit the ground and the grenade went off. They came out all right. There was a man who was little bit slow in things. He was made to carry a live 88 shell in front of him and run when he could not run anymore and his arms got tired, he was allowed to crawl. If they were good to him he was allowed to crawl on the gravel hill up and down which the striped suits had created. I often wished that one man would drop that grenade and blow himself and the N.C.O. up. That would have been a blessing for the man. We had it hard but him they just tortured him to the bleeding point. I didn't know whatever became of him later. The time we had been in the firebase was 9 weeks and we were credited with 8 planes shot down. It was a small satisfaction.

This time at Hohenfels, things were different. We had our own guns and halftracks. We were stationed here only a few days to get to know each other a bit. We moved out, motorized, to a place called Burglengenfeld, a small town in southern Germany. Here we were quartered in the schoolhouse. As we were a field unit now things had changed it was more relaxed. It took some getting used to hear that the NCOs were just with you. The only training we had was a bit more on the Panzerfaust. As it was discovered some had put the exhaust on their chest instead of over the shoulder when pressing the button. This of course killed the shooter. He was burned by the rocket exhaust. Next door to us in the other classroom they had the 60 meter type and everybody had to demonstrate how to do it. Everybody said I load, put the sight up, press the button and the Panzerfaust goes off. He was not kidding. The charge went off inside, the exhaust smashed the window, the head knocked the door out and knocked the door across the hall out too. Here was our office where they cleared out fast. Nothing could happen as the head had not contacted steel. Anyway it was quite something. We thought at first somebody had fired our 88 outside.

We waited in this town for rail transport to the front. We loaded in 2 days. We were on this train for 5 days. To travel by train was just plain loud and just about suicide by now. I of course had to man the machine gun again. It was the first day. In all the travelling we were never attacked. Civilian trains were always being chopped up.

On the 5th day we detrained in Stettin and with us was a train with approximately 25 Panther tanks. It was said we would be in action together and give Ivan a hard time. We could see that they would have made a powerful fighting unit. In the end the tanks were sent in alone and we were sent in alone contrary to all the fighting experience. Things were just not normal. In Stettin we stopped on the outskirts and I heard that my father was close by. I learned this information by mail from home.

On Saturday we had shooting practice again. I made out good. I had Sunday off and went looking for my father who was supposed to be in a land labor unit 8km from me. I found the place. They had just moved out. I followed to the new location. This was as far as I could go. I had not seen my father for the past 2 years and it was going to be another 4 years before I would come home to a new place in Mecklenburg. When we camped near Stettin it was just like home to me. We were let lose in the village and everyone took care of himself. Nothing was said about duty or where we had to sleep and it suited me fine. I went to the next town and bedded down in the hay. I had a friend from Vienna with me from some fine family. He asked where his bed was where he could wash clean his teeth. All things like that. I told him you just sleep in the hay and you don't wash. It was horrible to him. I had slept in the hay several times at home where I made it back late and mother was not supposed to know I had been out late. I just climbed in the hay and left early in the morning. I hid the bike in the bushes in the garden as our stalls were all locked by this time at night.

One problem was that Jahn, our tenant, left early in the morning and he spotted my bike. The rest he figured out when he saw the hay door partly open. In the evening he had to tell mother. What a spoilsport. So, sleeping in the hay was no problem to me. Others had found the distillery in the village so it did not take long to have some men drunk for 3 days solid. Those who dared were not bothered. Next day we could be out on the front line and who was going to bother anybody. We had a few N.C.O.'s short in the unit. Next day 2 replacements arrived. One was the drill Sergeant from Munich. I made a point to say hello to him. He was very friendly, but also very uneasy. He knew he would not survive the first engagement. He was so right. We trained for tanks. Both of us were to be proven right a few days later.

In this village in a few days everybody got lice. I did not get rid of them for one year and by the end of the year my chest and the lower part of my legs were eaten and scratched raw. One day I was detailed to ride on a truck to get supplies. In a big magazine there was absolutely everything we wanted and did not have. I requested a leather sling for my rifle because up till then I was carrying the rifle on a piece of string. Such was the case of the German equipment in 1945. At times uniforms were issued with dark spots in the cloth this was blood poorly cleaned. Units had airborne blue and army grey mixed. We were told the war was going good and just hold out a little longer and some wonder weapons would do the trick. When Fredrick the Great of Prussia was down he did not give up and it happened that he was saved. So Goebbel's minister of propaganda was hoping for a miracle again, as everything else had failed.

In a few days we were to move out before though I found out that

I had a leather sling on my carbine. Since all the others just had string it was visible. They made a federal offence out of it and I would be dealt with later. The later never came. Next day we were put on a train in Stettin and while we were in the east I had an idea where we would be going. There was only one rail line open and this was the one through my home town of Belgard. I started to hang around with the officers and as faith had it I picked up the words Belgard and engine change. This was enough for me. I knew it would take at least 2 hours before we reached Belgard at the best traveling time. I went to the closest Rail switch house and asked the man in the freight yard to phone my sister in Belgard. He was not sure if he would get through, but at this time everybody tried to help everybody. In normal times he would just have turned me down. Fortunately I was able to speak to my sister. I had just time to tell her I would be coming through in about 2 hours and we would stop for an engine change. What a coincidence, it was just like my father used to do 4 years earlier phone ahead over the rail phone. My sister phoned the railway in the village and in no time mother was on her way again to the station this time to see her son.

What a miserable time it had been over the last few months. One day at noon we were stopped again in the open and word got around that Dresden had been bombed. The result 100,000 killed we heard the next day. Nobody could understand this. I had seen Dresden a few months before and it was a lovely city. It was a city to see as it had not been bombed and everything was intact. I myself felt real cold anger as I had not cared much about other cities, but Dresden to me was different.

In Dresden were defenseless civilians the planes found to be an easy target. We all had been in many raids and knew that in a grossangriff, like Dresden did. It must have been horrible for the civilians. We were pretty cold to everything at this time. When some heard 100,000 killed they could only think that there would be 100,000 less people to feed. We all knew food would be scarce in the weeks to come and while food was constantly on our minds the conclusion was understandable, 100,000 fewer mouths to feed. The day after we heard that Dresden had been bombed again. Some must have had different information because they came right out and said Dresden has been wiped out. Die stadt Dresden existiert nicht mehr (The city of Dresden doesn't exist anymore). As on the other day we could not understand it as we all thought the war would be over in a few days never mind weeks. As with everything, our business lay ahead of us and we had no time to think of Dresden. It was just another catastrophe of which the 3rd Reich had experienced many and the last one, the unconditional surrender of the Wehrmacht and the splitting up of the Fatherland, was soon to come.

In February and early March we were on a train transport from Augsburg southern Germany for several days. It was supposed to be a 2 day transport to the front, but which front we were not told as the west was quite close we thought it would be the west. As we were on the train the 2nd day we heard that the Ivan had started a big offensive in the east nearby on the whole eastern front. Our train was often delayed as the city ahead had been bombed one time we thought we would go through Berlin but somehow we were detoured and after that we knew we were going East as we were going to face the Russians. We were a military transport all our guns in open railcars. In all the travelling no enemy plane came near us.

On the way to Belgard from Stettin it was not at all like I had seen years ago. The pine forest was full of people living there in covered wagons. The road what we could see was plugged endless with covered wagons drawn by horses. Everything and everybody was moving towards the west. The old rumor had sprung up again that Poland would go to the Oder river. So everyone wanted to make it at least to the Oder. The treks as they were called were endless in the east. They had escaped the bombing over the years but this was worse flee from your home in front of the ever rushing Russians. The atrocities and brutal acts the Russians had committed while entering Germany had spread throughout the east like wildfire. Nothing had been safe from them. Whoever could, packed up, and left towards the west. The covered wagon trains I saw stretched for 300 Kilometers toward the west. From west of Stettin to Danzig On the end I saw these wagon trains overrun by Russian tanks. What a tragedy. The tank commanders did not bother to fire and clear the street. They just smashed in and crushed anything in their tracks. Be it human or animal everything was crushed to death. This I had seen before and we were able to put a stop to it. The slaughter had ended for the day. From the phone call, I just made it back on the train as it was already moving. I placed myself on a half-track and had a good view of everything. It was the end of February, not too cold that day. As the train came near Belgard I placed myself on top of a 88 gun because I knew I had a chance for a look to our house from the railroad if I was placed right.

It worked out that way. I had not seen the house where I spent my first 16 years in quite a while. Rolling into the station in Belgard, my sister had done a good job of informing all the people who knew me. I was waved at from both sides of the tracks. I spotted my mother and sister on the railway sidewalk. The train stopped and I was partly home. Mother thought I looked kind of lean, but I was in good shape. The station had 5 tracks, on 4 were trains with people going west, but we were going east. People liked the looks of the SS as they knew they would have a breathing space from the Russians as long as we were behind them. Mother asked me if she should pack up and leave too. For the last days wagons and all types of POW's English and French had passed through our village. She traded with them for soap. By this time a population of 8 million people was fleeing to the west. Nobody wanted to face the Russians. Goebbels had said, "Victory or Bolshevik chaos" on big posters. It was going to be the latter.

As I left the station, I could not tell mother to leave. I had seen enough from Stettin along the line and could not figure out where she would go. Luckily my sister had things arranged just for such an emergency. She was able to secure 3 seats on an army truck and my mother left with 2 suitcases of useless things from the place where she had lived for 49 years. She never made it back. Never saw her home again. Where I had gone to, I would not be back for another year and a half. She would not see me for another 3 ½ years. Such is war. Before I was 20 years of age for one whole year I had not set foot in a house. Not slept in a bed. Not had a solid roof over my head. I had not eaten from a plate not sat down at a table. I had eaten out of a tin can with a spoon the can held between my knees as I sat on the ground.

Chapter Ten: Russian Tanks

We continued on by train to Lauenburg. This was the place where I had been in camp for 6 weeks and now I was back. The surroundings were quite familiar and the next day we went out digging holes for the guns. I had to dig a hole for the tripod and binoculars because as a plane spotter all guns were adjusted to the binoculars. The glasses were 10 x 80. It was based on a compass and all 6 guns adjusted by my reading. In the end all were aligned to the same number.

The company commander was not so sure about the surroundings as he came over to see the set-up. I told I had been in the area 6 weeks and we were on an awful spot for defense or pull out. Bush was on all sides and to close. We moved next day.

At night we had seen the red glow in the sky from fires. By now there was only one way left. Go on to Danzig where the war had started in 1939 because our back was cut off as the Russians had reached the Baltic Sea shortly after our transport went through. As we pulled back towards Danzig, the roads still full with covered wagons, they had no place to go. Infantry marched on the side of the road. They were Volksturm with no rifles, but a Panzerfaust. It was an endless stream of misery. In the afternoon some wagons broke out of the street and started going across a field. How they knew the Russians were on their back I will never know. We were still there. Then I saw the first one of our halftracks going off the road across a field and we followed.

We had gone off the road after panic broke out and seeing the fleeing people. Somehow they had got wind that T34 Soviet tanks were on our heels. We stopped and took position on the farmhouse grounds. For many of our 2-88 gun crew this would be the last position they would take because few of us would survive and see the day's sunset. We were behind a row of pine trees at the farm buildings in quick position. The gun was lowered but not detached from its carrier, just in case we had to withdraw it would only take 30 seconds to get mobile. While I was behind the house to look at our halftrack the Russian T34 tanks came out of the forest as the fleeing masses on the road

Above: a Canadian film crew examine a knocked 88mm gun in the anti-tank position. This is the same type that Manfred served on. (NAL)

had heard and we could confirm now that the T-34 tanks had only been 2 to 3 minutes travel time behind us. We were still aiming and our aiming scope was 6 degrees out.

All of a sudden we hardly had time to get into position when the Russian tanks started to tear through the fleeing wagons on the street. Things became a holocaust. Tanks firing point blank into all the wagons horses breaking off in all directions. People were yelling and screaming and it was just awful. I thought this lasted for a long time. It could not have been though. We took only 50 seconds and were firing away with the 88. We stopped the Russian tanks from the massacre of the civilians. The fight from this position was short and fierce. The tanks we could see formed an endless line like the last one was at the Ural Mountains and was just pushing ahead. We had two 88's in a good position due to our battle experienced commander. This was a lot different from the labor service. This time we could feel we had an officer who knew what he was doing. We saw the tanks at a distance of about 500 meters. At an intersection the wagons had all been overran as some tanks had the element of surprise and confusion on their side. Our first shot aimed at a Stalin tank was a hit. But it glazed off and went straight up into the sky leaving a fiery trail. The next one 2 ½ seconds later knocked him out and he burned a long time. By now the T-34 tanks with him had our position made out. We came under very heavy machine gun fire. It did no damage. It just prevented us from firing the 88.

I wondered where the halftrack had gone. Someone told me behind the house. This house was an older type made of clay and straw with a thatched straw roof. With the house was a barn that I found empty with just some straw on the floor. In the yard was the usual cellar for this region. It was a 10 ft. square hole in the ground covered on all sides and top with heavy timbers and sand more or less like an earth bunker. I wanted to see the half-track behind the house but was torn on deciding to stay with the gun or go on behind the house. While I was halfway towards the house I looked back to the gun about 10 meters away. By now for some unexplained reason and my feet carried me behind the house, even I felt like I did not want to go there. Just having a look satisfied me and all this took no more than 2 minutes.

From here I could see our 3.7 firing at the infantry who had come with the Russian tanks. This was about 100 meters away from where I was. The next moment I saw all the men from the 3.7 taking cover. It was not too late. Their gun flew through the air from a direct hit from a tank grenade. However, none of the crew was killed. The gun commander, an experienced N.C.O., had spotted the tank coming at them. A 3.7 was useless against a tank so he saved the crew at the right time. On my way back to the gun I heard something going by my head at a terrific speed. I looked back and there was a fair size hole right through the house. We were under gun fire from the tanks.

By the time I was near the gun a grenade hit. The gun was okay, but it killed most of our crew. Men I had spoken to less than two minutes ago were on the ground all their belly's ripped open the guts all on the ground. Some had no head, one had half a head and the other one no legs. Mostly they were just ripped apart. I remember looking a long time at the spilled guts. I had never seen anything like it before. It all looked purple greenish and dark blue to red. It was death on the field of honor. A long way from descriptions like he was killed in action. Everyone I had been on the halftrack with 20 minutes earlier was dead. Why I had an urge to go look behind the house even though I did not want to go is a mystery to me.

I heard my name being called by Captain Hauptsturmfuhrer. I did not even know he knew my name as I had only seen him on 2 or 3 occasions in 6 weeks after meeting him. I was not really on the gun detail anymore, but he knew that I was well trained as a loader. My specification was aircraft identification. What my commanding officer wanted from me was to load the 88 gun for him. He was sitting at the aiming sight and told me when to shoot.

The gun next to us was still firing and it was easy to hit a tank there were so many of them. By now they were stopped and could not break out. The gun next to us fired a few more rounds and after that she was hit by a grenade. The only casualty on the gun was one lightly wounded. The gun leader had only 3 men manning it. We were still firing. As I was the loader I just jumped up put the shell in and got down again. Aiming was up to the gun leader as he was the most experienced. He knew his business well.

We did well for about one minute as we fired 6 aimed rounds, got 2 tanks then the 34 tanks got the better of us. By now our company commander wanted to pull back. Just then we were hit by a grenade on top of the gun. Firing was finished. A hit on the hydraulic barrel leveler put us out of action.

We did not have many survivors. We blew the gun put 2 wounded on the halftrack and drove off. A few 100 meters the driver stopped and said the universal joint was broken (Classified as Sabotage). We dismounted and started walking. This was a good thing and in no time we came to a steep ravine where we would have gone down with the halftrack. Whoever could not walk of the wounded we left behind. As soon as it was dark we made our way out of there as by now the Red Army tanks had long bypassed us. The group commander for the 88 told me to salvage the aiming glass which we had not left with the gun and I was to make sure it got back to the rest of our battery intact. The weight about 9 pounds. I carried it exactly 100 feet and threw it away. I had lost all my personal gear and he wanted me to carry the glass. I could not see that. Fighting had come to a stop by this time, it was dark and all we heard was small arms fire.

After our short fight that we lost with the Red army tank guard division on March 10 1945, most of the crew of our 88 gun was wiped out. This was our first confrontation with the Red Army tanks.

The battery Captain said let's wait till dark and we will disengage and go to Danzig which was the only place left to go anyway. Some wounded must have heard this and now they called Kamerad nimm mich mit (Comrade, take me with you). If any one of us heard this or paid attention to it, it was ignored by all. As Waffen SS soldiers we all knew what would happen to an SS soldier if he got captured alive by the Red army. We all had one bullet in our pocket to avoid capture. Besides all the Kamerads if the German Wehrmacht had found a hero's death in the battle of Stalingrad. After this battle, the name Kamerad was changed to Kumpel. A name taken from coal miners. With this name, you were not obligated to anyone. As in our case we had been together in the battery for 3 weeks and hardly knew each other and Kamerads we were not. As we left, those who were not able to walk were left behind. I for myself saved nothing just what I had on. All my kit was left behind and lost. My mind was set just to get away from Ivan who we called the Russian. A sorry story indeed.

The line held here for the next 3 weeks and we had saved a lot of people. What a panic it was. What a mess to die in a war. The infantry which had dug in front of our guns had left long before we did. In the campaign in France in 1940 we heard one time German troops had advanced 40km in one day. On the day we pulled back the Russian tanks had likely advanced 60 KM in one day. We only pulled back about 15 KM.

When I came to the SS I was 17 years of age. So were all the others I was with. Our training was only 20 Days just enough that we learned to follow orders. At times we were in Munich guarding bombed out houses. Within 5 weeks we were in a fire battery on duty when the RAF or the US 8th Air Force came over to bomb the city which was quite often doing these times and we were at the gun for hours at night. Morning call was then 1 hour later. Usually we walked around like zombies so worn out. The year 1943 I remember when I was still at home there was not a day that I did not hear one of the boys I had gone to school with but a year or 2 older that they had given their life on the Eastern front for the glory of a greater Germany. I believed all this from the big losing battle at Kursk in Russia. We heard nothing but that all the losses were there. The Nazi party which we all followed had to rely on us 17 and 18 year olds now to stop the Red flood from the East. We could not do it. Today I think differently about all this. What gave Germany the right to devastate Europe for 6 years from the Mediterranean Sea to the polar circle and from the Atlantic to the Volga in Russia? The Germans could never justify this. It was the end of them. For myself my thoughts were that no 17 year old boy should experience this in his lifetime.

We made our way towards Danzig during the night. This was the place where our Headquarters were. It was not easy to find everything. I was with a friend of mine from the training days. We were both 17, but wise to the ways of hiding. For the next 5 days we traveled back and forth from Danzig to Gdedingia 2 cities 25 KM apart. The 3rd day in Danzig it got hot for us. The Russian 17.2 long range artillery was constantly shelling the city. There were explosions all the time. Once we walked along the street near a Nazi office. We saw 2 Gold Pheasants just ahead of us. They were called Gold Pheasants on account of their colorful Gold Braided Uniform. The next moment both were dead. An incoming shell had blown them right through a store window. My friend looked them over as they were still kicking so he took the Walter pistol from one of them before he was stiff. That's how we were at 17 years of age. In a short while more Gold Pheasants turned up. One noticed the empty belt holster. He asked us if we had seen who had taken the pistol and we said that we had seen nothing. He did not expect us to be SS men. Our overcoat was closed. He wanted us to help cover the bodies which we did not do. A few days earlier our friends had not gotten buried in the field and now he wanted us to take care of Gold Pheasants who were the absolute root of all this evil. We learned quick. Never have any scruples on anything when it served our purpose.

We reported to a collection station in Danzig and asked for the whereabouts of our unit. We were told no SS were in this caldron as it was now. The perimeter held. Mostly, it could not be held together anymore on account of all the people inside. The only way to make room was to kill people off or ship them out. The killing off worked very well. The shipping out not so good. Not nearly enough ships to hold all the masses of people. In Danzig we saw busses with all the seats removed and dead people piled inside like cordwood. All wrapped in paper and some had a tag on their toe. The busses toured and collected people in Danzig all day long. What a difference from 1939 when all the people here jubilant to be incorporated into the Reich.

One evening on our way back to Gdedingia (Gotenhaffen as the Nazis called it). We stopped at a house and wanted to sleep there. In the house were two women about in their 50's. We asked to sleep here. They told us they could not give shelter to any soldier as soldiers were to be the front and any civilians found harboring solders would be shot. This was a new law we had not heard of yet. We did not care, we slept in the house on the floor. During the night we heard the Russian shells coming in again. One was quite near and the next one blew the side of the house out. It had landed in the garden. This side was the women's bedrooms and all of a sudden they were looking at bushes near the bedroom.

The 2 women made it out of there and from then on they slept in the cellar. The next shell went well overhead. We had figured that and just went to sleep again on the floor. Next morning we left. We thanked the women. Mrs. Oliva Wolf of Danzig. They claimed the Poles would not do them anything as Danzig had been a free city before the war and it would be again. It was not going to be that way. I am sure we had left a good breed of lice inside the house as both of us were just about carried off by them. We had plenty of lice. We found our unit HQ in the afternoon and were quite welcomed. We were listed as missing in action, but it was just a matter of finding the unit. We stayed there for the rest of the day and next morning we were told where the battery was. It was about 15km from this point. We were to walk to them. We started but were in no particular hurry to get to the front so it took us 2 days to walk 15km. At noon on the first day we stood over at a slaughter house. This was a solid building with a good basement. It would stand a direct hit by the Russian 17.2 shell. The shelling never stopped. Whenever you saw one close to you, you were all right. The next one would be off. If it was off times you better find a hole to crawl into as the next one would be close. The shells dropped about 80 to 100 meters apart. In the basement of the slaughter house were hundreds of people, a real mixture, Poles, Germans, soldiers families with children. The place was just full with frightened people. The Poles offered me some food. I don't know what it was. Maybe borscht. Some mixture cooked in one pot. I did not eat from them. I remembered 1939. I gave green apples to the Polish POWs now it was the other way around. We left this place in the afternoon and went further up. Here it was quieter. No firing no explosions. You just heard the different sound of the shells going over your head. In the Gulf of Danzig was the German cruiser Prince Eugen. This ship was firing at the land targets far inland. The shells were easy to tell. They made a sound like a bus going by. You could hear them for a long while coming. I always thought I would be able to see one flying by. I never did. The Russian 17.2 gun was not quite as noisy.

Up at the front you were able to pick up anything you wanted. Howitzers, all clothing, grenades of which I took a few. I also put on a Russian step vest. This was real warm. I wore it under my greatcoat. The lice multiplied after this. I also found a blanket which I needed during the night. By the second day I was close by my battery. I had already talked to some friends. I asked for my old drill Sergeant. Everybody knew him. He had stepped on a mine the day before and blew himself up that way. I had in mind shooting him, and I would have done too. On the way to the front where I picked the grenades and blanket there was a body of an N.C.O., who was recently killed.

Lots of my friends were no more. The last few days had taken a heavy toll. Things were surely not going well and while in Danzig I had heard people quite openly saying so. The big wigs started the war and the little people had to suffer. This was quite true. None of them had more than the clothes on their backs. They had worked hard all their lives and now when they became openly outspoken they were strung up on the next telephone post by some Gestapo men which were still around. I have seen people hanging from every post in this region.

We got news of new orders. Orders always seemed to come through to the last man. Any soldier without his rifle would be shot. Any soldier running over to the Russians or his family at home would be shot. Everything ended with "would be shot". Such was war. People did not fight for a cause anymore. They were fighting just to stay alive. Up front we dug another foxhole every day. In the afternoon we wished it was night. After midnight you started to see things and shoot at anything that moved. We heard that opposing us were Germans from the Segoylitz army. These were Germans solders who had been turned around by the Russians. This was possible because the Nazis had only been in peacetime 6 years 1933 to 1939 and the communists were not dead yet by far. At night we heard singing from the Russian lines. It had a very demoralizing effect on us. I would hear them sing again later. It would not bother me then. Next time it was on the river Elbe and the war was over.

Every time I heard the Russians singing it was further west. From the marshes to the plains of Poland to Danzig and finally on the river Elbe. In 1949 on my way back from the UK, I stopped over in Berlin. One time I was in the east sector and here I saw a Russian squad of about 30 soldiers marching through Berlin and singing as they marched. I had always visualized myself someday as an SS man marching in Moscow. Now seeing these Slavic Russians in Berlin was too much for me. If I had a 1942 model machine gun I would have started shooting. The Russians singing in Berlin stuck in my mind for years. I hated them.

We had captured some Russians. They were quite up to date. We heard from them every second German has the Iron Cross and every Russian soldier has a machine pistol. How could we argue against that. One thing we did have, our rear command was good and food was good and plenty. Not like in the labor service. Here we had a rear with experience all around Danzig, the inroads had tank barricades. It was said they would stop the Russians for exactly one minute and 10 seconds. One minute laughing at it and 10 seconds to drive through it. One day I looked at this whole mess and could not see a way out. You were not to be seen near the harbor or ships as a soldier unless you were wounded. It did not take me long the catch on to this. One thing I did not want to be wounded so that I could not walk. But my mind was made up I was not going to die for the Nazis. I absolutely hated them by now.

One morning after shooting had been heavy all through the night, we came across a German machine gun nest a little ahead of us. He got involved at times too. This was the machine gun M.G. 42. I was trained on this gun, had often fired and liked it very much. It was a good killing machine. It got you out of mass attacks by the Ruskies as they were at times in 1943. This morning for some reason, I did not want to hang around. I was near the rail line and road crossing and I spotted another foxhole in a short distance and found that to be a better location. Once I got there I saw at once that I had made a mistake. This foxhole was near 200 yards of open field from the Russian line.

I knew from 1943, the Russian sharpshooters would waste no ammunition on a target like this. Perhaps that is why it was empty. The one ahead of me had seen the same flaw. I went out of this hole and at the same time, I got hit with a sledgehammer blow. I was hit in the hand and the back of the left foot. The hand was the worst bleeding. The back of the leather belt had saved me. The foot was not broken but very painful. The shrapnel is still there as of this day. I knew I was good for shipment out.

The first aid station just dressed my wounds and I was ready to go. I knew exactly where I wanted to go. It was the big ship I had seen days before in the bay of Danzig. I had about 20 kilometers to go. In my condition, about a day and a half. This I knew was too long. While I was standing on the side of the road, a Volkswagen jeep came along. I did not have to waive him to stop. The driver stopped on his own. He would not have gone far. I would have shot him out of the seat. Here was the law - a soldier was not to be without a rifle - to my advantage again. The way it was now, save your own skin and survive was most important to everyone now anyway. In the back of the VW was an army Major. He was sitting on the left side. That was wrong of him and to my advantage. I took the seat to the right and put my Mauser across my knees and the muzzle was pointed right at his belly. He asked me where I had come from. I told him Rahmel. He had a map in his coat and claimed that place was not held by German SS troops.

I was sharp at this time. I was not concerned what or who was at Rahmel. All I wanted was the ship ahead of me. With his remark Rahmel was not held by German troops, I knew he had not been where a Major should have been. After this I just told him (not asked) where I wanted to be driven. I had opened the collar of my greatcoat (overcoat) and when he looked over again, he wasted no time in leaning over to the driver and telling him to go to the Westerplatte. He was safe now too as he was transporting a wounded back. This major knew a lot about the ships. He told the driver exactly where to go. It was a large house near the docks. When the VW jeep stopped the Major just said to me "See - in there". With that, he and the driver were gone. I went into the house within minutes.

I was processed and like in any army, told to wait. The wait was only 2 to 3 minutes. An N.C.O. came along, relieved me of my rifle, and just said to go. He did not say where to. I could see the ship and as my rifle was turned in, I knew I was home free. When I went on board, the Major from the VW jeep was still there. I think he traded a place on the ship for the driver and himself. I was placed in a bed in a cabin, closed my eyes and as far as Danzig was concerned, it could be called anything after I left.

Near the ship there was something like a quick first aid station. The doctor looked at me said 4 weeks to heal up and be fit again. So I had made it. On the way to the ship I handed my rifle in and now I knew I was home free. On board the ship were nurses and I was early enough on board to secure a bed in a 4 bed cabin. Once in the bed I did not move till we were in Copenhagen 3 days later. This incidentally was not the ship I had seen getting loaded. The one I had seen was the Wilhelm Gustoff. A K.D.F ship before the war. It had seen good times taking German workers to all different places. The day we left with our ship the Potsdam, we heard the Gustoff had not made it across the Baltic. It had about 12,000 people on board when it was torpedoed and sunk with about 8,000 people. Some were saved by small boats. After that disaster we had a destroyer escort. The war more or less started for me in Danzig with the Shelling Holstein training and it ended for me in Danzig with the Prince Eugen firing overhead.

It took us 3 days to make Copenhagen, Denmark. At one time the nurse came and asked if anyone wanted to give up his bed. She had a heavily wounded soldier on the floor in the corridor. Nobody moved. Years before she would not have needed to ask. The wounded soldier was king and he had the best. Now the state was such if you were in the dirt nobody helped you out of it. Pity was a word unknown by now.

Our ship carried about 11,000 people. All decks were full including all corridors. Once you were on board and had a place to sit or stand, you moved for nothing and nobody. Once in Copenhagen things looked brighter because the Danes came to the ship with all kinds of cake they traded for tobacco. I had some and traded it for cake I had not seen this for years. Really well made too. From the ship we were put on a train the same day. The train moved out in a little while. Organization here worked fine. Apparently the train had been waiting for the Gustoff. As it was sunk, there were 8,000 less people to take care of. We had that train. Once on the train and in the west the worry about planes started again. In the East we had not been bothered by planes. It took about 2 days on the train to go to Salzwedel in the middle of Germany. We had not been attacked. It was marked as a Red Cross train this time. In Salzwedel this must have been the first week of April 1945. I was put into a converted school that was now a hospital.

I was on the second floor as I could walk. This was the first bed and house I slept in after 7 months of dirt. We newcomers had left our gear in the hallway. It did not take long and we heard a commotion. The man in the lower bunk asked me where my gear was. I just said in the hallway. He advised me to get it. I went out to the hallway and here already the vultures were at work. The other wounded were going through our belongings taking whatever was useful to them. It was no use telling them to get away. They had the same thing happen to them when they moved in. This was what the German Army had come to and the war was still going on. One man who had come with us was not going to have his clothes stolen. He had a good reason. Nobody had his pants off yet. He got hold of it and he had a pistol hidden inside. He cleared the corridor in one second flat. Everybody had respect for a barrel. All tried to save their hide and just get to the end. I got all my clothes. In my pants I had a good gold watch. It was safe. The watch I had picked up as booty.

Time was good here and I had lots of rest. The only work I performed was searching for lice in my shirt. I never gained the upper hand. In the hospital it was just a question of when this would be over. One day I went to a movie. I did not like the Newsreel because Goebbels was on again and compared our soldiers going to the field as to going to a church service. It was unreal from what I had seen. I left half way through. His words later became famous if there was such a thing for him.

Every day we had good news on the radio. The Americans were not far away. We knew approximately which hour when they would be here. Then one day I looked out and the whole street was decked in flags. All flagpoles which carried the Nazi flag before now had the white flag of surrender. The city was declared open. No shots were fired and the Americans moved in very carefully at first. On the first day we saw none. Then on the second day their convoys of war material rumbled through the city. Here we really saw material. Lots of us wished we would have had that. I walked away from the front window and very quietly. Our hospital had been surrounded by American soldiers. They looked very clean and tall. They had the helmet on the ear and awfully big pockets in their uniforms. We really liked their pockets. Everybody pointed them out. Just imagine all the food we could have carried in them pockets. We looked their equipment over real good. We were talking to them within 10 minutes. The helmet was half used as the steel helmet because they had a liner you never had to carry the steel helmet all the time. We did not like the back. Rain dripped onto your neck. Jacket and pants were new looking and good quality with big pockets. The boots were really good no hobnails you walked on rubber soles and they did not give you away. We didn't like the rifle. It did not match ours. The machine guns they had were too heavy. We did not think that they never carried anything. They had a jeep to go to the washroom.

Within the hour an American officer and a doctor came through the hospital to see it. It was a genuine hospital and all had to show their wounds as far as possible. When this was over the guards were removed and a notice posted on the door. We were prisoners of war. For me it would last nearly 4 years. What a relief that we had made it out alive. Everybody was happy even though the war was not over yet. Everybody heard more good news on the radio. One day president Roosevelt died and we were not sure what the Americans would do. Nothing happened. Everything went like before. Then we heard that Hitler had killed himself and a new head of state was in Flensburg, but the war still went on. We hoped it would end on the 4th of May. Then the 5th, the 6th, the 7th and it finally ended on the 8th of May. All of us in the room were glad it was over and that we had made it. It had come down to just making it. We had all different men from all kinds of former units in the room. Some of the older ones caught on right away. One older man was from Southern Germany. He started to curse the Nazis the moment they were out. We did not speak. The 3rd Reich was finished and he realized it right away. He went on like this; how those bastards should be slaughtered as they stole so many years of his life. Oh did he ever curse them. We were stunned but he was right. Before, such talk would have gotten you shot for treason. Now nobody even talked back to him.

Part III: From Tanks to Tea Cups

Chapter Eleven: Prisoner of War

A few days later, a U.S. officer came to our room who could speak and read German. He looked at my plate on the bed and marked it. He also marked on his sheet the number of wild rumors about me because I was the only former SS man in the room. In other rooms they had marked all the other SS men too. Plus 2 from the paratroops. Everybody said we would be picked up and shot. Goebbels propaganda even worked well after his death. Everybody had a cruel story. Next day we had word to be ready for transport in a half hour. As I was going to be shot I gave that gold watch to a man I had become friendly with in the room. Half an hour later we saw U.S Ambulances in the yard. All Negro drivers. We went down and they joked at our expense but of course we did not understand it. We found out we were only 4 to an ambulance. Everybody had a bed, no sitting, and we were to be really comfortable. All the windows were crowded with faces as everyone wanted to see what was going to happen to us. Well, they saw it. After a while we started up and we left with no guards just the drivers. We went out of town quite slowly on the open road and they opened up. On top of that the road surface was so badly broken we thought the driver was dodging planes. We were not used to so much power in the motor of an ambulance.

We soon learned what America meant. It was more than we had

been told by German propaganda that Americans can only make razor blades and refrigerators. Both articles we could not even get in Germany. We traveled for about 2 hours and then were let off in a town called Grifhorn. This was a bit further to the west than Salzwedel where we had left the others behind. Days later, Salzwedel was in the Russian zone. The Americans had pulled all SS men out of there and transported them to their own zone. All the rumors about us being shot were just not true. We were the lucky ones because we had made it through the war without ending up in Russian hands. I did not mind at all.

In Grifhorn we saw some English soldiers in groups of 3-4 on nearly every corner. They were quite pleasant. They showed us a newspaper head line that said only 2 words, `Hitler Dead'. I guessed what it meant. The news and the 2 words, one of which I guessed, was really the end of the 3rd Reich for me. I had seen it come and I had survived it. I was 18 years and 2 months old. The horror I had seen at this age I did not wish on anybody. I had no vote when it started and no vote when it ended. My ordeal in connection with the 3rd Reich did not end until 4 years later. In Grifhorn an altogether new life started. People were not so depressed anymore. They realized the war was over and it was lost. At the hospital we talked to the U.S soldiers. He showed us how to recognize their unit and ranks. The corners of the shoulder patch identified the army. Officers ranks were so simple we could not believe because it did not have a lot of silver. This was not at all what we had been used to.

The soldiers also explained the future zones of occupation to us. Grifhorn would go to the British zone. One day a big truck came into our yard and then 2 more. They were loaded right to the top. What they had was food rations because our kitchen was to be demolished in 2 days because the U.S officers had found not enough food could be prepared in the kitchen for the wounded. This was because the hospital was a converted school and overcrowded. For 2 days we were on U.S Army rations. Big cartons were delivered to our room. We counted and counted again. It was one carton per man per day. We had a feast. For the first time in my life I had chewing gum. I was not told not to swallow it as I had done with the first piece. Some cans we did not know how to open. In the end it was like Christmas in May. For 2 days we had a party; after the kitchen was done, food was plentiful and we enjoyed it as long as we could because it was said the English would soon take over. It did not take long to make this happen. Nothing changed. Food was cut down a bit but what mattered is that it was good. The guards first came in a Universal Carrier. They soon saw how idiotic this was so they pulled out after 3 days. With the U.S. guard we had handled his rifle while he smoked. I got better and realized I would soon be transported to a camp. The Sunday we had asparagus, but I never made it. The pick-up came just before noon.

I rode on a truck with a guard because we were 4 really fierce looking soldiers. Along the way the English got lost. They had German maps and the red lines on a German map went a different road than on an English map. In the end we made it to Gorleben on the Elbe River. This camp was just a big wooded area and where everybody stood. That's where we had dug a hole and that is what we lived in. The hole was 6 to 7 feet long, 4 feet deep and it had a foot thick dirt cover, which kept the rain out. The roof was covered with some tree trunks and branches before the dirt was put on. In all there were 15,000 men living in holes. I joined 2 men in their hole for the next 3 months. Work was none. Food was 6 potatoes a day. They were lined up by size and every day in rotation another man picked the first row of potatoes. So everyone had first pick in his turn. When he thought the 3rd or 4th had the best potatoes, he could kick them. He did not need to pick the first row. I laughed when I saw potatoes on the ration card. Here it was a matter of survival. The camp was surrounded by one fence of barbed wire, which was not much. We left the camp at will. We always came back because where could you go without papers? The British had good administration knowledge. All they did was apply their Colonial knowledge to their zone and they made it work, no matter if Germany was a colony or not. It was the only thing that worked.

Across the Elbe were the Russians. As in earlier times they had a singing concert in the evening. The only difference was it did not bother us anymore. One day, I believe it was in July, it got awful dark at noon while we had to dry wood to boil the potatoes. I took all the wood into my hole to keep it dry from the rain. As I expected it got a lot darker. The birds stopped singing in the trees and everyone braced for a rainstorm. No rain came. It was an eclipse of the sun.

A few days later we were transported off to a camp in Munsterlager. This is in the Lunenburg Heath. The camp was set up in the forest with all big tents and 50 men to one tent. It was better than a hole in the ground. Inside this camp was a smaller camp again enclosed in barbed wire. It was said that the Nazi big shots like Hess and Goring would be kept in here. In this camp we were former SS men only. Mostly men from the Wefer Abtailing 500. These were men who fired the V2. They had some kind of an overalls uniform made of good material. The camp had 3 fences of barbed wire. Every tree was removed for 20 meters along the wire. All grass cut and white sand covered in between the fences. Watchtowers plenty. One Englishman sang all night. We cursed him because he disturbed our sleep. I talked a lot to the men from the V2 unit. They did not tell me much, just that they had fired 18 on one day. Other day's only one or two. In this camp, we heard that the Atom Bomb had been dropped on Japan and Japan had surrendered. Peace was in the world at last.

Because we had to deal with the English, classes in English soon sprung up. One teacher was quite good. He had been to America. I did not attend his class because he asked for one potato a day. He had about 10 pupils. I listened to him at times and heard him talk about Detroit. I never figured I would see Detroit in my lifetime.

While we were supposed to be all SS men some claimed they were not. They had no tattoo under the left arm. Others burned themselves to obliterate the tattoo. It did not matter. The older ones soon got released, especially when you were in the British or U.S. zones. There were always some who believed everything they heard.

One day we went to a de-lousing station. It was wonderful. We had a shower and our clothes got washed. My clothes had not been washed for over 3 months. The tent camp was soon broken up and we came into some barracks in Munster. This again was better than a tent. It was winter by now. We received no coal to heat the barracks with so we cut trees at night. The barracks were warm after that. I had cut trees a year before on the Hasenberg.

We realized we were all young men. The sorting out had been done by the English quite neatly without much notice from anybody. Their experience and planning had proved to be good. One day we heard we would be moved again this time the rumor was to Belgium. Who ever lived in the west disappeared the night before. They had a home to go to so it was all right with us. We did not mind. The next day our troop was less than a half its size.

The rumor to Belgium was true. We left Munsterlager one evening. Next afternoon we were somewhere near Berbain in Belgium. This was part of Flanders. We hated it the moment we set foot on the ground. Here a camp was called a cage. We were back to a hole in the ground. Not just earth this was clay and mud of Flanders. We got very little food. The first day we were there, an English Sergeant came into the cage with a big colt on his side and we were told that his patience had come to an end with us. It would be tough going from now on. What we had done we did not know and were not told. Christmas 1945 came up. It might as well not have been. Somebody said it was Christmas and we believed him. We had a good present. One apple per ground hole and we were 13 in the hole. We had a guy with only one leg in our midst. He got the apple because otherwise it would not do anybody else any good anyway.

The next day we were moved to another cage that had 10 men to a hole. Food was for 4 men: 16 ounce bread, some margarine, one apple a day after a month and one quart soup a day. It kept you alive. You were hungry forever. The sheets we could move at will and moved in all directions. Then one day school started. However, not too many attended as you were too hungry to think. Your brain always thought of food. Trading in tobacco was good. I got caught once by a local policeman. He took all my tobacco. I got it back a few days later and I got even with him 2 years later in Scotland. A friend of mine knew our cage leader from home. He made sure I got the tobacco back. It was traded for bread. After this incident, I was called in by the chef in the kitchen. One day he asked if I wanted to wash his clothes. Was that ever a good job. A hot fire, warm water and extra food was good. I had it made if it had not been for the lice who by now had eaten me alive. Half my chest was raw, my legs all clothes bloody, I hated it.

For any infraction punishment in the cage was 28 days in the stockade. In the stockade was a pile of coal about 600 lbs. small bits and pieces you had to carry the coal with your hands to one corner of the stockade the other men for the next corner and so on. Always in double time for 10 hours per day. You usually lasted one week. When you collapsed the English sergeant would kick you back to your hole with his boots. One guy was given 28 days, just for taking a tent peg.

A day in a cage in Belgium consisted of waiting for food and the waiting again for food. The living place was a square hole in the ground 3 feet deep. This hole you shared with 15 others. At night you could sleep on one side like sardines. Morning tea was at 7 after that rest. At noon you had waited for your soup since last night. After the soup rest. At 4pm Bread and jam. Nothing to drink. Bread was weighed up on a homemade scale. Sometimes a square of bread looked gig. But the weight was okay. I hardly went out for 2 months. The hole in the ground was just horrible in the winter. Nobody washed for all of February 1946. Once a week we saved one pint of tea. We had one razorblade for 16 men and the tea was hot and good for shaving. One of the men in the hole could not go to the washroom for 30 days. He was finally taken to the hospital. Others used the washroom once a week to every 10 days.

All of us had come through a bout with dysentery. The time in Belgium did not do us any good. The ground became a real marsh in March. We did not go out of the hole as your shoes got stuck constantly. Nobody had shoelaces anymore. Some had no shoes. They used wooden boards with straps. By the end of March, our clothes had not been washed for over 3 months. Such was the state we were in when we left for England. My weight was 117 lbs. Usually I was 180 lbs. It was no wonder that the guards in Bury were given a hard time by the population.

One day we had to line up and everybody was given a sheet of paper with a name and number on it. I still have it. My number was A585329. We were told this was important. In future we would have to report by number. With the number we were easier to keep track of. A few days later back to the lineup. We got a needle of some kind. Some said the needle would break as they were too skinny, the needle hit the bone. One needle giver was an English doctor. He asked about the lice. I had mine now for over a year. The very next day we saw some of our men running around with masks on. DDT had arrived and the lice were finished that same day. This was really a relief. Now we were clean. The doctor came back. One more needle.

The rumor mill started again, but it had no time to get going, the English were too fast for that. We were loaded on trucks and onto ships to England within hours. They had planned well.

Chapter Twelve: England

The ship was not much. We were about 800 men. The guards were English shore patrol. Blue Caps. The crossing took about 8 hours. We landed in Tilbury docks London. Once in England things changed. The Blue Caps were gone. A train was waiting at the docks we landed up in between a freight train and a nice passenger train. The guards said to get on. We all got on the freight train. We were on the right track as we had always traveled on freight trains. We were chased out in no time. We were to go on the passenger train instead. We did so and felt comfortable with lots of room. A guard was on one end. We liked it because the train was clean and it soon moved out. Word got around that there were cigarettes under the seats. It did not bother me as I did not smoke. Others did so for the first time in months. The result was they got sick. By the time we left the train in Wolverhampton it was a mess, no seat was in place, everything full of vomit and it started to smell. It was in no time that we got out. Train change was in Wolverhampton. This was different coaches. I sat across from the guard. When he had his sandwich he gave me half of them. This was the way I was introduced to English sandwiches.

When we got off the ship at the docks in Tilbury we were told to form 2 lines. If you had a friend, which everybody had, you naturally walked side by side. Some by chance walked behind each other. The ones walking behind were the lucky ones. Here at Tilbury was an English trick waiting for us which we had not encountered before. Nor did we think ahead as everything was quite bewildering the first hours on English soil, and none of us had ever dreamed of setting foot on English soil as a P.O.W.; if at all we would thought we have been the conquerors. But now at last we were on English soil. As the 2 lines formed up at the ship and we marched out. All of a sudden we came upon an MP who split the line in the left and right one and if your friend was not behind you this was the last time you would see him as each line went to a different train and a different destination after that. Some men had been together ever since they had joined the now defeated Wehrmacht. They had been in the same airplane bombardment, fought the same Russian tanks on the Eastern front and many were trained together on the same gun. Both had got away from the Russians and had made it to the west to be captured by the U.S. or English forces. Both had survived and they came out of the war as comrades in the truest sense. When you had a friend like this and you had survived the war, you were glued together and had good hope to make it with him till the end. This meant until both of us would be back in the fatherland again. If one had to eat so did the other. You shared everything, your water, the tea, your razor. There was never any question on who owned what. In Belgium you both hungered, froze and hoped for better times. All this ended in Tilbury, but before we knew how to react it was too late. You had made it to England together like you were told during training in the Wehrmacht. But the result of making it was shattering. It was more or less the same as if your comrade had been killed next to you. I myself was in about 10 different camps in England, but did not meet with anyone I had lost in Tilbury. After this, it never worked again. When we were told to line up in 2 we knew what was coming. If the Tommy tried another method we made such a commotion that who ever wanted to be together stayed together after that.

We were detrained in Bury. From the station to the camp we marched through the city of Bury. Here we heard from English civilians the word concentration camp. They said that we looked like skeletons because none of us had been out of our clothes for the past 4 months and they looked as dirty as cardboard. Our uniforms had fitted us well in the Wehrmacht, but what we had been through during the last winter had made us look like inmates of the ex-concentration camps which everybody knew by now. The English guards with us looked really smart in their uniforms and we were obviously a stark contrast to them. That's why we heard the term concentration camp. The English civilians blamed the guards. They figured the guards were to blame for our condition. Later there was an inquiry in the House of Commons but by that time our ordeal was over. Most of it was blamed on English officers (Rapid Change DE mob) and also the Sergeants. It was too much for them. But by this time we could not care less. We were out working and stealing whatever was not nailed down. We were detained in Bury in the midlands on the way to the camp. The English guards were threatened by people in Bury since we looked like skeletons from the hard winter in Belgium and the people thought the soldiers were guarding inmates from a concentration camp. Our uniforms were not much to look at anymore and we looked horrible.

It was not far to the camp from the railway and it was an old factory. This was my first day in England. I liked what I saw. People were just like us. Once I was in a working camp, it did not take long to establish contact with the people.

In the factory there were other German P.O.W. and it was partly a working camp. Work at this time was strictly voluntary. Most worked as it included some benefits. Others we saw in their full German uniforms with all decorations. We could not understand this. They were living in another world. The English did not bother them. They could do us no harm. Here you had a bed and a mattress for yourself. This was the first time I had a bed for myself for over one year.

Besides our regular food, we received ½ a loaf of bread and 1 quart of porridge extra a day. Nobody came near us the first 3 days. Then on the 4th day it was nice and sunny. We were called out in groups and when we came back in, they had changed our uniform from German to English. On this day we went to another part of the factory and there were some English soldiers and one officer. The soldiers were supposed to search us. This was only partially done. Whatever we had in terms of momentos from the German army this was the end of the line for it. I did not go to the search right away. I looked it over as I had my army book and I was not going to give it up. By the time it was my turn, I had figured it all out with the search, and the book was still mine at the end. (I still have it to this day). After the search you walked a few feet here you got undressed you got rid of all your clothes the underwear stunk and the pants and uniform jacket was so grimy it stood up on its own. It had not seen cleaning for 1 ½ years. In other words we were all glad to get rid of it and put on something clean. This was a luxury for us. All was English army issue. Khaki outfits. The pants had a diamond patch front and back in the legs the jacket a round patch on the back. The patches were of different color usually red or yellow. Some years before I had seen how the Germans marked the poles and Jews with patches. Now I had a patch myself.

With new clothes - even if they were English - I felt really good. The next day we received a whole extra bread. It had been donated by the civilian population of Bury. They had not forgotten our sight as we marched from the railway to camp. Every night at 5pm was roll call in this camp compared to once a week in Belgium. The ordinary soldier never at any time was able to get the count right. By 6 pm the Capt. arrived. It was about 6.05 when he saw us still lined up on the parade ground. He came counted once and within 2 minutes we were dismissed. After about 10 days, we were detailed in some groups of 50 men and the next day we went to another camp. This was about 80 miles away and was an all working camp. By now we looked a little bit better but were not allowed to work. The food here was just good. As a working camp most of the P.O.W. didn't have much need to eat, but the kitchen had quite a bit of surplus food especially with porridge every morning after the others had left for work and we got another helping. I usually had 3 quarts of porridge in the morning. Then 1-2 more around 10 am. At noon the bread ration with bits of margarine, jam, cheese. In the evening a hot meal. Always lots to eat. Some days we ate 5 quarts of porridge in the morning and others gained weight so quickly you could see it every day.

We had all received 2 sets of new clothes a week ago. In this camp we sold one set of clothes the day after we arrived. The P.O.W. which went out to work sold everything to the Englishmen outside. I had a pants with no patches. It was worth 6 shillings. Later, I found almost everything we sold brought 6 shillings. For the money I bought cake which we called Tommie Cake. The cake was real good. I also got some Cocoa. This I used to mix into my porridge. We had porridge with the raisins, porridge with Cocoa with sugar or with salt. After 2 weeks of the porridge it came out of our ears.

This camp was real good. It was an old U.S. army base built in their style comfortably, even a shower and library reading room. We had come a long way, but it always got a bit better. This life lasted about 3 weeks. By that time we had been divided again into groups. I left from here to the south of England (Hampshire) to a working camp. This camp had 500 men and was near Bulford, which was administered by the war department. This was good for me. Other camps came under the department of agriculture that was mostly farm work. War department work was better. Bulford camp was an army base. The few civilians present belonged or worked for the army. In this army base the Southern Command H.Q. was located. We had nothing to do with that. Our camp was 3 miles from Bulford in tents. Not in the ground. Everything was well landscaped.

The main buildings were all Barrack style. Good compared to what we had lived in and had put up with for over one year. In this camp after a week we had a medical and were asked if we wanted to work. Most opted for work. Pay for work was one shilling or (12 pence) a day. 1 ½ pence an hour. By the week you had 6 shilling. 6 pence was withheld for the camp personnel as only outside workers were paid. Also, in case of sickness this paid you too. In camp there was a barber which we didn't have for 4 months by now. We did not start work right away as we were still recuperating.

Two weeks later we started to work outside. I was detailed to a group of 5 others. A truck picked us up outside the gate and took us to Bulford. My work was in a scrap yard for planes. In this yard were all kinds of planes. We broke them up and pressed the parts into a square block with a machine. It was clean easy work. We scrapped planes for weeks. Years later I heard there was no Spitfire to be found anymore. We must have done a thorough job because sometime later I was detailed to another group. This group marched out in the morning to Bulford and it was easy walking through the Salisbury plains. Fairly flat country. The work was painting girders and parts from Bailey Bridges. First paint colour was red and then green. I did not paint well. I did not care anyway and beside I had always heard a prisoner does not do a good job for the enemy.

One day I was doing my usual bad work. Up comes some other man and gave me hell and asked me what I thought I was doing. He said I should clean up my act as the work had to be perfect. I listened around to hear who he was and was told he was a self-appointed foreman of the gang of 30 and he had been a Sergeant in the German army. This was all I needed to hear. The next day I booked off sick. To start with I did not like the marching out in the morning as it reminded me too much of the army days. Then the ex-sergeant giving me hell. That was all too much. This being sick did not suit me much either though I did not like outside work as I had no contact with the English and no chance to learn English. So I opted for inside camp work.

I had found that I had no trouble learning English. Camp work was mostly cleaning up or helping in the kitchen. One day I got into an argument with the camp warden. He went to the office to complain and on the next transfer to another camp my name was on the list. A transfer was not what I liked. I had been with a good bunch of men most who had been with the SS Hitler Youth Division and they had served under General Major Meyer in France, which were a really good group to be with comrades to the last drop. Really good. From these men I heard for the first time of the carpet bombing they had lived through in France. Not once but twice. In the East we had only heard about carpet bombing passed down through several men. Here I heard it firsthand.

They all claimed that it was absolutely the worst. Most of them went crazy after they had survived the bombing. All spoke very highly of Meyer (Meyer was in Canada 2 years after the war). The Allies could not prove much against him so he was let go. When I left the camp, I did so with a heavy heart. I was truly sorry to part from these men. I had heard the new camp was 40 miles away in barracks so it was an improvement after the tents. The camp was in Westbury. Really good. Barracks were good. Food excellent. The camp was on a main highway and there was always something to see. This camp was a lot better than the last one. Work was ½ mile away at a big supply depot. The depot had originally belonged to the U.S Army. After the war it was turned over to the British. In this depot was absolutely everything an army needed; from food to beds, uniforms, laundry. Nothing was missing or in short supply. Everything was piled up to the ceiling in long tin huts. The depot was so big I had never been to all the huts by the time I left. We worked 5 ½ days moving equipment, which was ordered from the English Army to where ever they were. Fridays you could always see groups of men going to one of the huts. This was the clothing hut. I and all the others never washed our underwear. Every Friday we broke open a box and dressed new. This we did for weeks. Anything we wanted was no problem and was new.

We never actually stole anything. We always dusted it off or organized it. It was the same as stealing. We did not care. If we wanted it, it was ours right away. What could the English do to us? The worst they dreamed up was 14 days in camp. We stole everything and if it could not be stolen we destroyed it. A while later the English locked the huts with big padlocks. They lasted exactly 3 seconds and we took the door out with the lock. We hooked a chain or rope to the lock and pulled the works with a truck. This one man climbed up the pile of stacked boxes and kicked the top box down. Everything we wanted was down by our feet. If we were too lazy to climb we used the fork lift truck to smash boxes. One day a military truck arrived with M.Ps and a Captain, very official. We had an order for a radio transmitter. A big thing. We were told the price. In 1945 it was worth $30,000 dollars. The Captain was not very polite. He saw us and saw red. Later we heard he was Jewish. In other words he did not like Germans much. We did not like him either. He handled his stick for everything and even poked us with it. He spoke some German. He made sure we understood what he meant. He wanted the radio set loaded on the truck in one piece. We could not figure out why he made such a point in one piece.

By the time we had the radio set near the tailgate of the truck we had figured out what he meant in one piece. That radio set never reached the inside of the truck. It slipped and we smashed into roughly 30,000 dollars of nothing. The Captain did nothing. He just stood there. He looked and opened his mouth as if he wanted to say something. He never did. He got his M.Ps and drove off. We heard later this was supposed to be shipped to Germany. To the English Army ft the Rhine. Now it was a pile of nothing. We had to paint beds for 2 weeks. What a punishment. During the bed painting time I went to the other huts and looked for things. I got in to the Corned beef 5 lb cans. Then Salmon lots of other things. Actually we did not need extra food or even other food. Our kitchen was good. We were a gang of 10 Bed painters. One English civilian as overseer. He had a supervisor and was really scared of him. He was an elderly man who could do no other work. So he always tried to please the super. We were always a good gang. Every day he took our name and number to see if he had the same gang.

In 1946 everything was still rationed in England. All the Englishmen were not allowed to steal from the depot or take anything home. Everyday this one Englishman asked us what we had to eat in camp. I had made good progress with my English and he talked to me quite a bit. I always told him. One day I said I had about 4 cans of corned beef. He could not believe this I assured him it was so. He must have known that I was in all the huts while I should paint beds. So one day he said he would pass by our camp on his way home. The control on the gate were really sharp and if they found anything they were fired. By now I had it better in England than the Englishmen themselves. Next day when he passed by our camp I threw him a 5 lb. can of corned beef through the barbed wire because he was a good man. Later things changed and I got something from him. I carried a 5 lb. of corned beef nearly every day into the camp. It usually rained and the can was on my back under the cape. Controls were nearly daily at the camp gate. We marched in threes. You just told the man next to you. I carry. When the soldiers pointed to you the next man would step ahead and as long as the soldiers had his 5 men to search he did not care that he had not the one he had pointed out. The Sergeant wanted to see 5 men searched and that was it. We walked quite fast in the rain and the first 3 rows were through the gate before the soldiers started to look for someone. We carried the works and no one ever got caught. The guards were only at the gate so it was easy to get a can over the fence.

We were about 300 men in the camp. We had a real good band and the music was superb. Later in the year we had movies. There were all English papers in the recreation room. In the meantime I had learned to read English enough to understand things. This year 1946 was the first time I had contact with the written word in a democracy. What I read some evenings in the

English papers was unbelievable to my thinking. It took me a long time to get used to this. By the end of the year everybody in the camp took an interest in the war crimes trials at Nuremburg. When the sentences came out, we compared the sentences and figured we should be out by now. It did not work that way though.

One day an intelligence officer as he was called visited our camp. He spoke to everybody one at a time for 40 seconds to one minute. After the talk you were classified 1-2-3. Number one would be sent home within the month. Then number 2 sometime after that. Number 3 was classified as a Nazi. In our camp only 2 men had number 1, several #2 and the rest #3. When I went in to see the officer I was asked, "what do you think of Hitler?" I answered him. Hitler is dead and that is it for me. So I got #3 Nazi. Even so I had never legally voted for him in an election. I was a Nazi in 1946. The #2 men were classified as anti-Nazi. The only way they could get this was by being a communist before the Nazis took over. A communist did not change his thinking after 1933, while a Social Democrat did so and joined the ranks of the Nazis. We all considered this interview to be a big farce. You were not able to appeal your grading. It was final.

Our main camp in Westbury had a hostel. It was 30 miles to the south with about 25 men. As some of them got repatriated I found my name on a transfer list one day. I was detailed to the hostel in Services. This was quite normal, last to the camp first to go on detail. I had heard about Services. It was supposed to be better than the camp I was in. This was hard to believe. We suffered no hardship and it was good. Services was better. This was a modern formerly U.S base camp. Nothing was small or old. Everything the best. We had one row of wire around the camp. But that was nothing. You could walk out at anyplace. Nobody did it. It was fair to good in the camp. We were not attached to the rest of the camp because it was an agriculture camp. No 25 belonged to the war department. We had it better. Our work was next door in a big storage area mostly uniforms. The huts again were full to the rafters. One hut was full of boxes with officer's belts made of real leather.

I was lucky. I worked in this hut with 3 P.O.W. and one English Corporal. His name was Bill. At one end of this big hut were Haversacks and we were supposed to pile them real nice in even stacks. Most of the time we threw the sacks at the Corporal and he fired them back at us. So most of the days we had a haversack throwing battle. The other 2 with me had come from the U.S. P.O.W. because instead of being sent home the Americans had unloaded them in England. The P.O.W. from the Americans were very rich. They had twice the supplies in American issue to what we had. Really good clothes. Both of them talked a lot to Bill, the English Corporal, about America. He could never hear enough. Bing Cosby was a big hit with them. Bill just forgot to work when they talked about him. Their talk was all in English and here I really learned the language. With Bill we had 2 hours for lunch. The Sergeant came at times, but Bill was on top of him. We always worked hard. Bill said one day we should not organize any of the officer's belts as the boxes were counted. We had no intention of organizing any. After he said it we cleaned several of boxes out. The boxes were still there but empty. All the outside boxes were full. We organized so many belts that the camp had 600 P.O.W. and every one of them had a belt. Then we sold the rest for the magic 6 shillings again.

Later we carved them up with nice designs on the belt and those sold even better. All men on the surrounding farms in services had belts made by prisoners. Of course we did steal from the

War Department. One day Bill came and told us when we leave the depot at noon we all would be searched. Not that it mattered to us. We went through the wire several times a day and took everything out this way. The search at noon turned up nothing. The next day Bill received a belt from us. He thought this was real nice of us to make him a belt.

We only had to go around the corner and we were in our camp. The others in the camp arrived by truck later. One night we saw a big gathering of soldiers at the camp gate. This could only mean a search from the returning P.O.W. We were right. The trucks stopped across the street on a lot and the barracks were always locked over before going through the gate, all the soldiers were hiding behind the guardhouse so not visible from the parking lot. We put up a big sign on one hut which read Filzung in German. Even if an Englishman was able to translate Filzung it meant nothing to him. As this word had been coined by the P.O.W. and only they knew what it meant. Nothing was found at the gate. Everything was left with the truck driver. He was a civilian Englishman he had to come back next morning.

Everything was returned by him. It was said the P.O.W. owned ½ of England. We had a lot. On Sundays we usually had a soccer game. All the lines were drawn with flour. The lines were real white. People were starving of hunger in the world, we buried the soccer field with flour. The work at this hostel lasted about 5 weeks. After this I had to go back to Westbury, the main camp. The camp had changed somewhat as some had been sent home. The barbed wire was only 6 ft high and one fence instead of two fences 12 feet high.

After proving our clothes had the red and yellow patches clearly visible, we were allowed out on weekends in a radius of 5 miles from the camp. Some went out, but I did not bother much. The barracks I had been detailed to on my return held only 8 men. This included one man who worked in the camp office. He usually typed the English orders in German for the Bulletin board. One evening he came in and just mentioned tomorrow I will put an employment bulletin for 6 men to work as officer's batman in an officer's mess. Where this mess was he did not know. He figured it would be a good job. One condition was that some English speaking was required. As far as I could see I qualified. I talked to him and just mentioned 20 cigarettes if my name was on the list next day.

Chapter Thirteen: Batman

The next day my name was first on the list. I left Westbury within 2 days. A truck took us back to the camp where I had come from the Bulford Camp. Here I had to wait a day and I was not quite sure if they would let me go to the mess job. I didn't exactly leave from this camp in good terms. I found out they had nothing to do with us. The only care we had from them was the doctor. The next day we left for Bulford. The truck stopped at the Southern Command Headquarters Mess. Here we moved into the Mess building 3 to a room with all comfort. After 1 ½ years in tents and ground holes I finally was in a building with a solid roof over my head. In the evening, an English Corporal came to us. He showed us some rooms and said to wake the officer in there at 7:00 am next morning.

We all did not know what to do next morning. The kitchen personnel and waiters for the mess were P.O.W. too so we got along with them. They did not know what we had to do either. They were staying in a hut a block away. The next morning we started work. I went into the room. At first I saw a uniform on the chair with all kinds of red on it. I woke the man and he mumbled tea. I did not know what he meant. He pointed to a cup on his table. I took this and went down to the kitchen and got a cup of tea. That was what he wanted. I had 3 officers to wake. They were one Colonel, one Lt.-Colonel and one Major who was a dentist.

The officers worked next door in the command building and started at 9 AM. We learned this in time. During the day the Corporal showed up again. He told us what to do. Make the bed sweep the room. Clean the washbasin, shine the shoes, press the pants and things like that. We soon settled into a routine and it was easier by the day. Weekends were off as most officers left Saturdays for London 80 miles away or to their home. Some did not go to London every weekend as they claimed it was too far.

All the officers had their own cars and some had 2. The Lt.-Colonel had a silver Jaguar. He, I found out, also had race horses. He was quite rich. This Lt.-Colonel (De Aubuz) spoke German quite well. He needed it at first to make me understand what he wanted. In general, all were real good gentlemen. The Colonel was tops (E.M.H Clifford) He was a real gentleman. All his clothes were handmade, the very best. There was nothing cheap about him. He was in his early 60s nearly retirement age. After a few weeks, he became friendly and we talked quite a bit. He wanted to know how old I was and where I had been during the war. He mentioned that he had been in France and when he saw German soldiers my age as prisoners he knew they had won the war. He was an experienced professional strategist. He knew you could not fight a major war with 17 year olds. He had also been in Ethiopia, India and Singapore. He was very nice to talk to.

The officers had a ration of cigarettes that were below regular price. He did not smoke. Later I got all his cigarettes.

One day he threw his uniform out. He had only removed the crown and pops and all the Red stuff was still on. It was very nice. One evening he asked me if I wanted his old uniform. He did not have to ask me twice. I understood him right away. I told him I would dye it, have the jacket altered at the camp tailor and I would show him afterword's what it looked like. I did all this at the camp that was 30 miles away. The only way to Westbury was by bus. We were only allowed 5 miles from the camp. I took the bus anyway. Before I left I put the Colonel's uniform with all the Red on the collar in a little suitcase so that the Red was on top. Travel pass was on top of this. I had seen the bus conductor and found that they were mostly retired soldiers. I figured if they were only half as scared of an officer as this Corporal who told us what to do they were scared enough. After about 15 miles in the bus the Conductor came to me. He wanted to know if I was a P.O.W. I said yes. Then he asked where I wanted to go to. I said Westbury and I had a ticket. He claimed I could only go 5 miles. He wanted my bloody name and number and also the camp I was stationed in. I told him Southern Command Headquarters, my name and number and then I opened the suitcase to show him my pass and I said he would have to deal with Colonel E.H.M Clifford whose uniform I had in here. All I heard after this was a lot of `bloody' and `Colonels'. The conductor did not come near me for the rest of the trip. The Colonels uniform had done it.

On the way back I had the same conductor and he never said a word, I just gave him the ticket to Bulford camp. The tailor in camp had done a real good job with the uniform and the Colonel did not recognize the suit after I showed him. After this I never wore a uniform with a patch again. If any soldiers wanted something from me I just told him go and deal with Colonel Clifford at Sothern Command. This always worked wonders. Several times I needed it. I constantly ignored the 5 mile limit. Colonel Clifford was good. I washed his car and took good care of him. I got good reference paper from him. After one year. Lt Colonel Dc Aubuz was more out for himself, but very helpful. He asked one time which camp I belonged to and if I had friends there. I said I did have friends in Westbury. He said he would go that way next Sunday and I should wait for him at 2pm in front of the mess. I was there 10 min to 2 as nobody was there by one Min to 2. I went back upstairs to my room. One minute after 2 here was the Lt.-Colonel calling for me at my room. He was a stickler for time. When I brought him his tea in the morning at 7 AM I used to wait outside the door. He had the Radio on the B.B.C and when the announcer said 7 Oclock, I knocked and served tea. This put me in the good books for the whole day. We went down to his car, the Jaguar, there was his wife—a very elegant woman - and I sat in the back and the Lt.-Colonel in full uniform drove a German P.O.W around. The world could not be crazier with him calling for me in an English Officers Mess and then on top driving me 30 miles to camp.

He dropped me near the gate on the main road and said to be at the guardhouse at 7.00 PM. I know he meant 7pm sharp not one minute before or after. I was back by 10 to and I asked the Sergeant if I could stay in the guardhouse until 7 because a Lt.-Colonel would come and pick me up and drive me to Bulford 30 miles away. He said sure and let me into the guardhouse. I did not stay in the first room as the Sergeant ordered me in the back room. I could see the clock from where I sat and imagined what would happen when the Colonel came in. Before that every soldier had looked at me so as to say we got one. At exactly 7 pm. I heard attention feet stomping. The Colonel was in the guardhouse. The soldiers pretty well were falling over each other. All I heard was, "YES SIR, YES SIR."

The Colonel just said to me, "come on Fred lets go home."

TEL: BULFORD 3171
EXTENSION 97

HEADQUARTERS
SALISBURY PLAIN DISTRICT
BULFORD
WILTS

31st October, 1947.

GUTZKE Manfred, P.O.W. No A585329 has been my personal servant for exactly twelve months. I like him personally. He is intelligent and takes an interest in his surroundings, and his work has been excellent. He has my sincere good wishes for his future.

[illegible]
Colonel.

Above: a letter recommendation for Manfred by one of his officers.

Right: Manfred at Southern Command Bulford taken by an English Major.

The expression on the soldiers faces including the sergeant could not have been more stunned. The Colonel and I had a good laugh in the car as he told his wife. The visit to the camp was very good and I had a few more cigarettes for the men who had managed to get me the job. I also received new information on the Red Cross Refugee Service. I was allowed one free postcard through the Red Cross. As I could not write home, I send this card off to the distant relative we had in Berlin. The lady I had visited in 1944 on my way to Czechoslovakia. It was now late in 1946.

I had no idea if anyone from home was alive and the last they knew of me I was on my way to the East. In February 1945, to my surprise I had mail one day. It was only a short letter written by my sister and it said they were all right but in Mecklenburg. They were very surprised to hear from me from England. They thought for sure I was in the East. Mail followed after this quite regularly. We were allowed 2 letters with 25 lines each and every month. The letters were not sealed. My mother had to write the familiar words `Prisoner of War' again.

A real Irony. I was well settled in with my officers and in a few weeks the Major took several pictures of me in front of the officer's mess. It was absolutely amazing how helpful and concerned they were. The Lt.-Colonel even gave me oranges which I had seen last in 1939 that was 8 years back. We still only made 1 ½ penny per hour. This was P.O.W. money, which could only be spent in the camp canteen. Most articles we needed were on hand. Oranges not. Maybe nobody would have bought them anyway. The only way to get English money was by working for them and asking them for money, but they were not allowed to give money to a P.O.W.

I cut the grass for a Lt.-Colonel who had arrived and stood over in the mess for 2 weeks till his family arrived. He moved into a 14 room Manson with a big garden in Bulford. He had 2 servant girls, one a cook the other one the nanny who was a real nice girl of 17 years. She and I were quite friendly. The Colonel had 2 cars a big 6 passenger Talbot and a 1947 new Ford mostly for his wife. The price in 1947 was 600 pounds. When I worked for the Colonel I never asked for money, but I asked his wife for combs, cotton, needles. I sent all this to my mother in Germany. Those were things she did not have and they came very handy for trading for other items. The Colonel's wife always wanted to know what I was doing with so many combs or cotton. I made 2 parcels and she paid the postage. In the Colonel's house I saw what it meant to be an officer in a nation that ruled an empire in the world. They had chests and carpets from India as the Colonel had served there. Also lots of other items, figures, lamps. He had quite a lot. All 14 rooms were full. He had 2 daughters under 10 years. After we were allowed a 5 mile walking distance from camp, I had been to the house of the man I had given the corned beef to. He had a garden with some vegetables. He gave me some tomatoes, carrots and onions. After all he owed me something so he said. Inside the house I was surprised how poorly he lived.

As Germany had no colonies I always thought that England with all the colonies was well off and so were the workers. The fact was very different. I found the ordinary Englishmen in 1946 had not as much as my parents had at home in 1938. He had only bought a radio in 1946. The U.S. Army had provided work for him in the depot. Clothes were good but very poor. Every free minute he had and in company with a few others they gambled tossing penny's on a wall. That, and going to a soccer game Saturday afternoon was all they had as recreation. In comparison, the upper class like the Colonel really belonged to the rulers of the empire. I believe the Colonel had a salary of 40 pounds a week in 1946. One day the Colonel asked if I would accompany him going fishing. I told him that I would like to but I could only go 5 miles distance and I did not want to cause him problems. He had never heard such nonsense. He said that he wanted me to go fishing with him and I went fishing. The river was about 20 miles away. Something like the Persante a river which I was used to. It did not take long and he hooked his line. I looked over went in and freed his line. This little deed really did it. He told about every officer in the mess. After that I went fishing and freed lines. His name was Colonel Hoblyn.

During one time that we went fishing I watched how he drove his car. The next day I took his car. Washed it and then took it out. I drove through Belford in a real good speed. I did this quite often. One day I came back from a drive and the other men were playing soccer off the street and I waved for them. I lost control of the car, went through a ditch and later I found the car had a broken spring. I knew this as the car sat a bit to one side, I said nothing just waited till the Colonel took it out. It just so happened I drove it out of the garage for him. He looked the car over. He said nothing. It was nice and shiny, 3 days later he told me he was in Lark Hill 5 miles away and had a spring put in. It cost 20 pounds to repair. I said nothing. Next day at the house he had a bicycle and said I could use it. I surely did I biked all over the place in Southern England. One Easter I biked to the camp 30 miles. At the gate the Sergeant blew his top at the thought of me going over 5 miles away. I advised him to see Colonel Hoblyn at Southern Command. He did not bother to see the Colonel.

The next day I left camp somewhere in Westbury and I made a

wrong turn on the end I ended up in Bristol. I was thinking of getting on a ship to Canada which I had heard of. Then I decided it was too far away. I tried to find my way home. This was not so easy. I was hungry and thirsty. I saw a milkman delivering milk. No chance to get a quart there was always someone nearby. I finally stopped at what I thought was a police station. It was a motor league office. Here I asked the way back to Bulford. I had to do 50 miles. One man drew me a map and gave me some of his sandwiches. I biked on and soon I was thirsty again. I went into a little restaurant. I had no money. I figured somebody would buy me something. I was right. I got 2 cups of tea paid for by some patrons. It was only a few pennies a cup, but that was the Englishman. After I left here I stopped 2 more times. Once at a house where I got some bread and tea. I felt just like the men who used to come to my mother's house years earlier begging. Next stop was a house and there was one man home. He made me bread and tea. While he walked around I noticed he was blind. I was very hungry and it would have been easy to help myself to bread as he left it at the table. I could not steal from a blind man. I made it back to Bulford. The others had covered for me as they figured I had run away. The Colonel did not say anything. He must have missed me.

The Major also allowed me to use his radio over the weekends when he was in London. Naturally the Corporal saw that I had the radio. Next day I happened to overhear from the corridor that he mentioned to the Major I had used the radio. The Corporal was told to mind his own business and I had his permission to use anything he had. Things were getting really good.

Twice I looked after a Captain for a few weeks, but a Captain was like nothing to me I was used to higher ranks. I treated them accordingly. One was a late sleeper. He had to be in the office by 9 am. I used to get his breakfast on a tray. I woke him at 10 min to 9 and said, "Sir your breakfast."

He looked at his watch jumped out dressed shaved and out he went. I sat down and had his breakfast. I knew it would be like this. One day this Captain was transferred and he packed his own gear. He forgot his dancing shoes. Real nice ones with mirror finish. I sold his shoes within ½ hr. to another P.O.W. after he was gone. It was 6 shillings again. Nothing was holy in the eyes of a P.O.W. The other Captain left his car out one Saturday. I knew it meant I should wash it. I did not wash it. About 12 noon I got called to the President of the Mess Committee. He was a Major. He wanted to know why I had not washed the Captain's car. I told him the Captain never gave me any Cigarettes and I would not wash his car. He looked as if he had not heard right. A prisoner telling a Major in the English Army, "No Cigarettes, No Car Wash." Then he got me. He asked how it had been in the German Army. If we had to do it first and then complain. I said it was so. He said it was the same in the bloody British Army so go wash the car and then complain. It was too late by now. I never washed that car.

One of us had the name of Vogel (BIRD) in English. He had been with the U-Boats. He was a batman to a Major who could speak some German. Whenever this Major wanted him he would poke his head out the door and call in German, "WOIST MEIN U-BOAT VOGEL." Where is my submarine bird. In general the officers were better to us prisoners than to their own soldiers. One Captain, a Jew, always tore his bed apart after I had made it. I could not figure out why. In the end he said he wanted his mattress turned every day. I said I would do it, but of course I did not. The next day, the bed was undone again. He said I had not turned the mattress. He showed me pencil marks on both sides of the mattress and the cross was supposed to go down today. I got a pencil and changed the cross. It solved the problem. We never had inspection in our room.

Next to us was Colonel Clifford. The men in the kitchen and waiter in the barracks had inspection once a week. Beds had to be done up English style. This was very strange to us as they had no bed sheets and this was one of lots of other things we did not like. Then one day it was announced the English soldiers would get bed sheets. They really made a fuss about this. We just mentioned we always had bed sheets in the German army.

The officers had to pay for their food in the mess every week. We had our own chef in the same kitchen. Our food was better than what the officers had. We came first. As I was living in the mess, I knew several plates were set in the dining room from Sunday night to Monday. This was in case of late returners so they could eat something. I went down to the dining room after midnight and took whatever I liked. The officer could eat the rest. Sometimes none came. The waiters had found only certain things were gone on the plates. The Chef asked me how I liked the officer's food. I claimed I never had any.

Every month or so there was a big party in the mess. One time it was really big. All the officers' wives were present. The Colonel and Major called me over and introduced me to their wives. We had white jackets on and served as waiters. Our Chef had outdone himself. He was a professional. His cooking and baking could match anything in the most expensive hotels in London. To this party he had outdone himself. The cakes were just out of this world. We were told to give it to the party first. Whatever was left over we could have. I had misunderstood I could have it first and the leftover went to the party. I carried whole cakes to my room. (I still hear about this now 30 years later, as I still write to a man who was with me in Bulford). I had all the chefs' best cakes and Tortes. For 3 days we had the best from the party.

While we were not in camp payday for us was every 2 weeks. The English Paymaster was a Captain. The actual payout was done by another P.O.W. One payday after the party the paymaster had not enough money. He could not figure it out. We were only a total of 30 men and he paid us more than 300 men in camp. He claimed a day had only 24 hours a week 7 days' time at 1 ½ pennies an hour. He gave a sum what we could have. Our day had about 30 hours. The week had 8 days and the Colonel had signed my time sheet. I advised him to see the Colonel and tell him he had signed something wrong. The Captain never saw the Colonel. The next pay day he had enough money so we didn't have to go to the Colonel and complain about the Captain not paying us enough. There was nothing we could not pull off. The call for the Colonel always worked. Later we had a Brigadier General at the H.Q. and our pay went higher. I surely made money here. So did the others. One time I looked after a Captain for a week who was a tie nut. He had a tie for every day in the year. After I was through with him, I had a tie for everyday of the month. Some of the ties I even took back to Germany 2 years later.

One day in the spring of 1947, 3 of us were called to the office. We were told to get ready for 3 days outside duty. This duty was about 80 miles away. It was a big demobilizing camp for English soldiers. The soldiers were here for about one week before becoming civilians. The 3 of us were to serve food at a big party put on by the Generals and other officers. Several big tents had been erected with long tables of food and drink. While in this camp for 4 days we worked exactly 5 minutes. I served one dish and that was all I had to do. We ate in the army mess, received bedding from the army and organized a whole barrack for ourselves. The soldiers in the camp did not like it at all. It was their last few days in the army and all claimed they had enough. In camp was lots of Military Police. Women got de-mobbed here too and fights between the soldiers happened every day. I never knew what the party was all about but it was a good break in our routine in Bulford.

One time I went to Westbury with 2 others as they had not ventured out too far. I showed them how to do it. Westbury was all right no problems at the camp gate. On our way back we had missed the bus someplace. We started to hitchhike back. One car stopped after a short while. The driver was an ex-army officer. He got talking to us in the car. He mentioned he had been in France. My friend said he had been in France and gave the town. It so happened they had opposed each other in France on the same dates. The ex-Captain drove us close to home and upon leaving gave us 10 Shillings. This was good for one package of cigarettes for each of us, which were 3 Shillings 4 pence a pack in 1947. This was another good example how good Englishman were to us. It was the same in the big depot were I worked. The English always claimed they were okay.

We could not go to Scotland unless we volunteered. All we had to do is say to the English in the depot that you would go to Scotland and he would tell you the most horrible stories from Scotland. We had heard something from other P.O.W., which had come from Scotland. They did not think much of it. I would find out someday myself.

All in the summer of 1947 we had a really good time in Bulford.

We heard the repatriation was going quite fast in the camp. Some of the waiters left the mess and replacements that came in were English soldiers or civilians. In Bulford I got to know a soldier by the name of C. Poole. We exchanged addresses and promised to write at least once a year. It is now 1977. We still write to each other.

I had nothing to complain about for the time. I had been alive. When we heard we had to go to the camp it was not welcome news, but lots of camps had already been disbanded Westbury had 2 at one time was now only one. This was the agricultural camp. When we finished the mess it meant going to the agricultural camp. This was a big switch for any one of us. I was one of the first to leave Bulford. The Colonel gave me a good reference paper and said he would be a civilian in another month. It was just as well that I left. In Westbury, the camp was as good as the other one even closer to town. I was detailed to work on a farm with some others. We graded potatoes and bagged them. Food we had from the camp. The farmer if he had any sense, supplied tea with cream and sugar. Tea alone he was grade 3. Tea and cream was grade 2 Tea cream and sugar was grade 1. He got good work. We bagged the potatoes well. It meant we did not add anything to the potatoes before we bagged it. Grade 3 had that. Grade 2 got the tarpon line cut which usually covered the threshing mill which was on the field. If we did not cut the tarp we put sand in the gears. The farmer was wise to treat us right.

He would not find the damage done by us till next spring and by that time we were long gone. The time was over where another prisoner came up to you and said, do a good job painting ... as it had happened to me over a year ago. We figured we should be home by now at the end of 1947. As we were not, our anger was pointed at destruction. We heard every day that things had gone wrong at places. Some of us worked in a tannery. This gang wore leather in camp. Others made real good wallets from the leather. The wallets were sold to the Englishmen at the tannery. They did not know or did not want to know that they were buying their own leather back. (I still have my wallet in 1977). One day the farmer gave us Black tea grading potatoes. He went to inspect his field and left the car near us. He never drove the car again. We had drained the oil. Next day this detail was finished. I went to another detail digging drainage ditches on meadows. Just like I had tried to help and had seen the Polish prisoners digging ditches in Germany in 1939. While working at these ditches it was said the last time they had been done was during and after the First World War. This also was done by German P.O.W. So here we were again, doing ditches. One thing I will say it was better than the time in Poland with the German labor service.

We suffered no hardship. When it rained we finished. While on this detail I had heard in camp that the Batman to the Commandant was going to be repatriated. My name had been mentioned for replacement. It was known I had experience from Bulford. It only took one week and I was Batman to the Camp Commandant. A Major did not fancy this much which meant some advantages. But it was nothing like Bulford. It was quite good now that I had left Bulford as one of the first. This job in camp opened up just in time for me. In all the years I was in England I worked on a farm for 3 days and on ditches for about 3 days. I was always lucky in job placements.

The Commandant had a dog which I did not like. The dog did not like me either. As Batman I also had to serve on the table at noon for the officers and I had to wash some shirts. The laundry I only did for a few weeks until I burned a shirt and that was it.

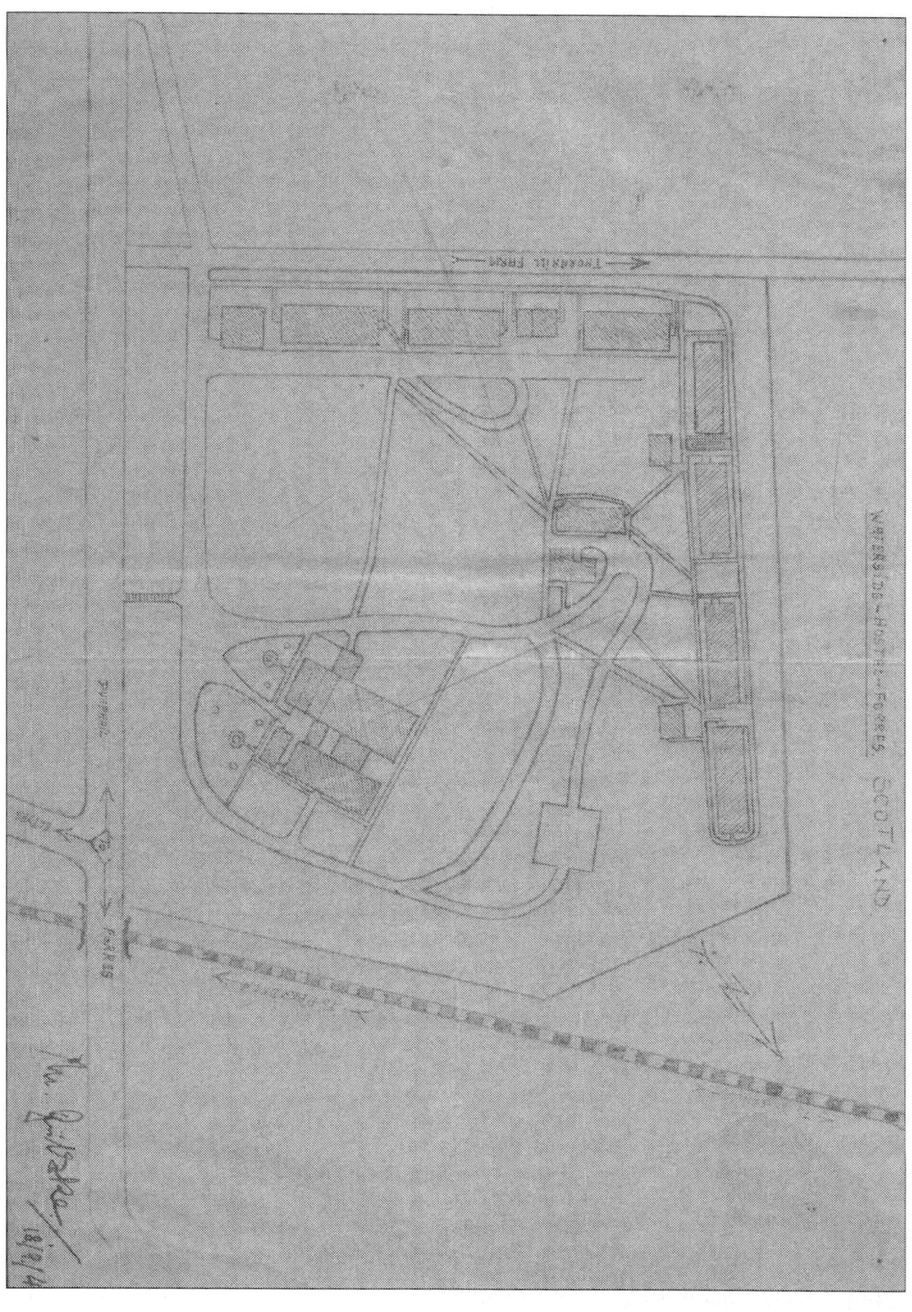
WATERSIDE-HOSTEL-FORRES SCOTLAND

I hated doing laundry. By now it was Christmas 1947. The Commandant gave me one pound as a Christmas gift even so I had burned his shirt which he had to replace. As a Major he only had 2 shirts and I burned one so he only had one left. He had no car. But a really good bicycle. He went home to Summerset by train. It was not far.

All the time the camp had become smaller. We all knew in January of 1948 it would not be long till the camp would be closed. In the middle of February we found a notice on the bulletin board which advised us to choose to go home or volunteer for farm work in Scotland. The camp would close in 2 weeks' time. I had no place to go in Germany so I chose to go to Scotland. Quite a number of men in the camp did so. No one had any trouble to prove that he had worked on a farm in England. Except me. I had to go to an interview. Here I said I had worked on a farm and the officer did not know my background so I was okay for Scotland. We left in a few days to a place near Plymouth in the south of England. Here we waited for others to join us. When we were about 200 men we went to the station and traveled to London. All the days prior we had good time to look over the City of Plymouth and Southampton. We had lots of money and time was just like a holiday. Transportation was all on the compliments of the taxpayer. While in this camp near Plymouth I was approached by another P.O.W. who asked me if I wanted to be his chief in the camp in Scotland. He said he would be the camp leader. I did not ask how he knew this. He knew and from that moment on I was his chief and became the boss of the camp in Scotland within 2 weeks of arrival.

On our way to Scotland we stopped in London for a day for sightseeing. It was capital city of the empire where the sun never sets. I had been through London once before when we embarked at the Tilbury docks. These docks are well known and they stretch for miles along the Thames River. The docks are used for shipping British to all parts of the empire. I would say every British soldier who served overseas knows Tilbury docks from one time or another. Now in 1947 I was back in this city. I was still a P.O.W. supposed to wear a khaki uniform with big patches of different colors on the back and front leg. I wore no such thing as others did not either. The Tommy's who guarded us or were supposed to, did not care. All they had to do was keep 90 P.O.W. and have them at their other camp. In London we had to change trains to go to Scotland to get to another station so we used the subway. To this day I will never know why nobody in the subway got separated. London was a very busy city. I should soon see more of it. At the other station we had to wait 6 hours for our train. This was too long for our guards and they said be back here by such a time. We all had English money and every one of us went in to London; a world capital from which a colonial Europe was ruled; a city which had a real King and Queen in a palace.

London to me was not much. At that time, it was better than all the city's I had seen in Europe the last years. Here was a city with hardly any war damage. People who lived here were in a nation which had won the war. Everyone, it seemed to me, was awful busy. I had seen pictures of London at home in books and always counted the streetcars and buses on them. It was these pictures all over again. I did not like London much as it lacked homes. Wherever I looked, big buildings, the sign of a capital which controlled trade and commerce in the empire and the world. It was the capital of a nation who had won the war in every sense of the word.

When we were back on our train station most of us had gone to see the palace. All were impressed by the buildings which ran block on block. It was a good break on a journey to Scotland. All over London and England I saw big Billboards asking people to work more efficiently. Things like cars as everything had to go for export. I found this rather strange as this was the country what had won the war and they were short all over 2 years after the war had ended.

Next stop were the midlands including Nottingham Forest. Here we received more clothes and got told and instructions on English customs. Most of us already knew how it was out of camp. In order to have some exercise we were led out on a march into the forest. We had taken no raincoats and as it started to rain we all ran back to the camp without the guards. On the gate the guards would not admit us to the camp. We waited till our guard Sergeant came by, but that time we were all soaking wet. This march in the rain had some repercussions in the Midlands. All of us had some friends by now somewhere in England. Most of us wrote to them complaining of the treatment we had received from the guards. I wrote to my friend C.A Poole. He in no time had a letter to the camp Commandant's office to find out why he had let us wait in the rain. I did not deserve to get wet. I was his friend. Just as I was to be interviewed by the Commandant the call came to board the trucks for the trip to the station. It was just as well. I didn't have much to say.

Our train ride to Scotland took a day and a half. As we got further north some wished they had never seen this forsaken land. Moors dykes and sheep not much to see. We stopped again in Edinburgh for sightseeing. Next day we boarded some local train for the hinterland. I forgot the name of this place and it is just as well. It was barren, windswept, nothing for miles from anywhere. Whatever we had heard of Scotland this was everything combined with a lot of nothing. We got our last instructions. Here were the last threatening words. The officer told us the very next day that we were not civilians yet and we could all be sent back home and if we did not like it we could step forward to go home. Nobody stepped forward. We all knew we would be out of here by tomorrow. It was that way. It could not have come sooner.

In this camp we were split up into smaller groups of 90 men. When we left here we were no more P.O.W. We were civilians and the commandant had nothing to say anymore. Now we were organized by the Y.M.C.A organization. I was in a detail for Forres and my appointment was confirmed by now as chief labor officer.

This Hostel in Forres was quite good. I had my own room, lots of authority and made a lot of money. It was five pounds and 18 shelling a week plus free board and lodging. This was more than most Englishman received in pay. The hostel was close to town. It was more than we could handle. Some of us got quite drunk. My job was to detail 90 men to work details in the surrounding farms and have 3 to 4 trucks leave every morning with the men. It was good work, good pay and had its benefits. While I was the boss in the camp, I had my hands full at times too. In the next few weeks we got our own trucks and drivers that we picked from our gang. We knew the country by now. One day I went with a driver to Dingwall 90 miles away to pick up some trucks. It was a nice trip. On our way back the driver just asked why I did not learn to drive a truck. I started to learn right then. Three weeks later I passed my first test for driving trucks in England. After the test I really made money because all my driving was on overtime. At times, the big boss came in and always took me along in the car to the farmers. We had to inspect the help at times. I traveled through the north of Scotland far and wide; all for free.

One time I was in Dingwall and came near a camp which had barbed wire around. This was 1948 and was hard to figure out why. In the camp were ex-Polish solders. They were still here as they could not go back to Poland. One of them asked me if I had any dollars. He said he would pay a good price for some. I did not have any but asked what he wanted with them. He said he had papers to go to Canada, but needed dollars to pay for his fare. Here was Canada again which I had heard twice before in my life; when my father spoke of the Canadians and when mother told me of the birth of the Quints in Canada. I talked about this in camp, but no one was interested. We knew we had until the end of the year to decide what to do after that. We could stay in England, go home or go home for 2 weeks and then come back to work on a farm in Scotland or England again. By the end of the year most of us opted to go home.

While I was the labor clerk in camp I had to know everyone. To my surprise I saw a familiar name. It was the one of the policeman in the cage in Belgium who had taken the tobacco from me one time. He recognized me too. I had my chance to get even with him. Whenever there was a farm miles away he was on it. He knew he had it coming.

The Scottish were quite easy to get along with. A hard working people in the year 1948 the Highland games were held in Forres and I had lots of time to see bagpipes and watch the games and highland dancing. The time in Forres went fast. I always had lots to do on weekends. I went to other farms mostly Findham on the North Sea. The Scottish liquor laws were such that you could not drink in your own town you had to be a traveler at least 5 miles and sign the hotel register. After that you could get drinks. Other times I traveled to the Sands of Culbine. This was a big area near the sea and was nothing but sand dunes. The story goes that under the sands lies a village that was buried during a card game which went on for a long time with a stranger.

In all, the time in Scotland was good to me. Others who worked on the farm had a tough going. The farmers planted potatoes on slopes where only mountain goats could walk. It was hard picking. Most of the time the frost came before the potatoes were out. It did not matter to the farmer as long as he made an effort to harvest potatoes. He was paid by the government for his loss. So much per acre. Not much grew in this region any way. Frost always came in late September.

During the summer months I managed 2 hostels. One was about 12 miles away and it was filled with about 30 Scottish students.

As long as they went out 2 hours per day they were paid a full day. One student claimed he was a driver. My boss in the region said to employ him as a driver. I pulled him out of ditches all over the county. One time I made a pickup of some men on a snowy afternoon. I went off the road with the big Bedford I was driving. The truck had 4 wheel drive and it pulled out on its own power.

By the end of October we all had enough of Scotland. Arrangements had been made over the last weeks to get us home. We left in November 1948 by train to a place near London. In this camp we waited till the transport was full for shipment to the continent. It was not long and the transport took about 7 hours across the channel. We landed in the Hook of Holland and boarded a train for Germany. From the train we saw other trains loaded with Volkswagen cars. They all went to Rotterdam for shipment overseas. The train stopped near Munster in Germany. Here we were asked where we wanted to go. I said Breilengen by Luneburg. I received a train ticket for this, 40 marks, and I was on my way as a truly civilian after 11 years. I belonged to no organization now which I had from the time I was 10. From now on whatever I did was on my own nobody directed me anymore. Just a free man 3 years 7 months after the 3rd Reich had come to an end.

Chapter Fourteen: Civilian in Germany and Poland

Brielingen, which is a little village, was where my aunt Tante Grete lived. She was with the teacher her daughter, Hertha, who was married. I had no other place to go and only had this address from my parents in Mecklenburg. I was not too eager to cross to the Russian zone of occupied Germany. While I was in Breilingen, I looked for work at a nearby airfield which was in operation during the Berlin blockade. I had not found a permanent place to stay in Breilingen. It was 20 KM from the next town and not what I actually liked. The teacher went hunting and one night he came back he claimed he had hit a moose with a 22 as he had not switched over his rifle to 9 MM. The next day we went out looking for the moose. I found it not far from where he said he had shot at it. This teacher was an experienced hunter and he knew he could bring it down even with a 22. The rifle belonged to the farmer in the village. It was highly illegal to go hunting. How could they? They supposedly had no weapons. In Lunenburg, every hotel had venison on the menu card. Hunting was in full swing. I also met the designer of the Tiger tank in this village who said he would design a better tank. I don't know if he was ever called upon to design another tank.

I could not stay in Brielingen forever. One day I went to Hamburg prematurely because on my return I got word that there was a message for me in Breilingen to come to Hamburg to a bank and pick up some money which was due to me from the time in England. The next day, I went back to Hamburg and received 360 Marks for my work in the mess when the week had 8 days. The pay clerk was surprised to pay me so much. He said the average was 250 to 300 Marks. He would not have believed my story anyway so I just took the money. This money would come in real handy at a later time. From Hamburg I went back to Breilingen and as I could not stay here any longer I left the eastern zone to see my parents. By now it was just before Christmas 1948. I traveled to Lubeck by train and the streetcar to the border. I could have passed legally for the first time I returned. I had no idea how a border crossing worked. I heard so much that nothing made sense. Nobody I talked to had actually been across. In the end of the streetcar station I met a farmer on a wagon. He could see what I was up to. He asked me on the wagon and took me closer to the border. When I left him he just pointed to a creek and said that creek marked the border. There I was looking to the east and figuring a way to cross here.

I waited till it got dark then I looked a bit closer at the creek. It was quite deep. Nearby was a railway bridge. I decided to cross here. By this time it was about midnight. I crossed by the bridge, walked for another 50 MTR and ran right into 2 Volkspolice. I asked them to let me go home as I had only been released as a Prisoner Of War from England. There was no talking to them. They took me to a village named Herrenburg. In the village I was placed in a pig stall with some other people and nobody knew what would happen. Whatever it was the Volkspolice were in no hurry. I was lucky I had something to eat. It turned out that I had to stay in this stall for 2 days. On the next day I heard I would be interviewed by a Russian officer.

This would also include a search and I had to bring all my belongings. I had 2 suitcases full. All good articles from England. I also had 2 watches and the money which if found would be confiscated. Someplace I picked up a picture of myself in SS uniform in Munich. I took this picture and was just going to tear it up as my name was called. I put the picture in the coat pocket. The watch and the money I had placed in the fly of my pants. I had found in all searches in England in the camps you were never searched at the fly.

After my name was called I went into a room where I saw one Russian officer. He could speak fairly good German. With him were 4 Volkspolice, 2 behind a table and 2 in the middle of the room. The 2 behind the table searched my suitcases the other 2 went after my body. One put his hand in my coat pocket. He had the picture. I whispered in his ear to leave it in the pocket, but it did no good. He threw it on the table in front of the Russian. All were very interested in what I had in the suitcases. The Russian officer got hold of my English dictionary. This he was quite pleased with. He looked no further. He said something to the policeman and they stopped what they were doing and I was told to pack up. The Russian spotted the picture as he talked to the policeman. He looked at it looked at me then asked if that is your brother in Russia. I said no that is me. This was enough for him. I heard "verdamte (damned) SS". He stamped my release paper and yelled at me I should clear the room. I had noticed he had taken my English dictionary. I had the nerve to ask him through the interpreter for the book back. This was really it. I left the room fast after I heard him answer. Before I left he wanted to know what it was like in England. I told him very good. Just like the Western Zone. No pig stall for lockup in England. Now I have another English dictionary. It carries the remark the first one was stolen by a Russian officer. Someday I will write to the Russian embassy and ask for compensation because a Russian officer should not do such a thing.

In Herrenburg, I took the train to Klutz which was not far. I arrived at the place where my parents were living on Christmas Eve 1948. I had not seen my mother for nearly 4 years and my father not for 5 years. Since 1943. It was not much of a homecoming as my parents had only one room and a kitchen. They had 2 beds and some other furniture. My sisters were living there too. I don't know where they had got the bedding from. When they left our family home they did not even take cups and plates. One day a woman in the building that had been used as a customs office gave my mother one cup and a plate because she had found out mother had nothing. Everyone waited his turn then in eating from this plate. This went on for a few weeks. My sister Lotte had found a job cooking for the Russian detachment in the village. This job saved them from starving to death. My sister had the leftovers from the Russians in the kitchen. She also took the rest to Mother and Father. One day a Russian soldier saw her eating the leftovers. He asked her, "Frau Du Hungry". Woman are you hungry? What could she say? From this day on there was enough food at home. The Russian saw to that. At this time there was no home in Germany 1945-46 that did not experience hunger. The Russian gave my sister some plates, knives and forks. We had nothing at home. My sister told me later father had gone for days without food. But he did not say anything to mother. They found out 2 years later. It was a very hard time for them. On top of all that they did not know where I was.

Ration cards were issued but no food was in the stores. The little food that was at home father left for my mother. What a change to the first ration cards we received. Now not even potatoes were available of which we had tons at home.

The Russians had moved away from the village after a while. They went to the next big town. My sister had to go with them and cook. When I came home she just told me she cooked for the Russians and did not like it. She said they had changed. The fact was they had not changed. The soldiers had been replaced by troops from the N.K.W.D the secret Russian police. She cooked for them now in a house in town. My coming home would soon change all this. The Russians had to find another cook while I was with my parents. I asked about the people from the village were we had lived. I wished I had not asked. It was a horror without end what I heard. Many had been killed by the Poles who took over their homes and then refused to leave. If they were shot that was quick and easy. Most were clubbed to death. So was our tenant Emil Jahn as he could not tell the Poles what I had done with the 22 rifle I had. A Russian officer had set up office in one house and systematically interview all the people in the village. I had pity for the ones who had fled the Russian Revolution about 1917-1918. These were now the sons and daughters of the revolutionaries in Russia who caught up with them 25 years later. They did not escape their fate. The sons of the revolutionaries finished what their fathers could not accomplish with these people in 1917-18. One was to hand his sewing machine over. He refused. Both were shot on the spot. Man and wife buried in a hole in the yard.

Some farmers claimed it was their farm and would not leave. They were not shot, they were clubbed until they died. The next farmer left with no argument. In general the people were told to assemble in 20 minutes with 15 Lbs. of luggage in the village square. The search was done in a garden and here they were searched, the 15 lbs. was reduced to nothing mostly. If someone had buried something the place was raked by others from the village and it was found. After the search they were driven like cattle to the railway by the Poles with whips. You had your choice to run or get whipped to death. Most people just turned their key to the house over to the Poles and that was 40 years or more of work done with. Some of the Polish prisoners who had been in the village were working for farmers at the end of the war. They just took over. For a while the farmer who had owned the farm for years just like his father now worked for the Pole. In a few weeks everyone was driven out. My parents heard later that the Poles and Russians had been looking for us quite actively. They could not believe that my sister had managed to get mother and sister out in the last days. She had. The ones which were still there blamed everything on us. I had a rifle. We had a big Swastika flag. Father was commander of the Fire Brigade. It made no sense. All had signed their names in the Golden book one time. All had pulled for the Nazis especially the ones with big families as they had lots of baby bonus every month.

Now they denounced each other in front of the Russians. Such were the stories I listened to from my parents. All the farmers had done quite well under the Nazis some had a tractor others even cars. All had new threshing machines. The threshing machines were a big improvement after all the previous ones. I had seen threshing done in the barn floor. It was usually done by 3 people in unison. The machines threshed and cleaned everything in one operation. They were easy to take care of. They had to be kept well greased in all the bushings. The price was about 3,000 marks. A lot of money but a farmer could afford it. He would get 200 marks for a 250 to 300 Lbs pig, 800 marks for one cow and 800 to 900 marks for a horse. After the Russians had been there a few weeks all the women were rounded up and had to clean all the grease from the bushings. The Russians liked clean machines. After they were cleaned they were transported to the city, loaded on trains and shipped off to Russia where army transports were moving in 1939. Now the Russians transported farm machinery for days on end. Everything what was moveable was moved off to Russia. Later it was said that all the transports went as far as the Polish-Russian border. Here there were no Russian trains and the Machinery was just pushed off the train. The train had to go back to Germany empty.

Some people had seen broken machinery for miles along the rail line. Not all houses were occupied by the Poles right away. They were stripped and left to collapse. Most of them were burned down. The shoemaker across from our house was not able to fix shoes anymore for the Poles. He had no material so they burned his house down. In a way it was not his anymore. The Poles just burned property although they could take it anytime they wanted it. All they needed was a hint that it did not work and a rifle to shoot the owner. It was every possible way to drive the people out any way the Poles wanted to.

After a few days of this, I had heard enough. I started to look around for some work. In this village was not much to do. I went to the next city and applied for the Railroad Police. The officer there looked at my application and told me quite frankly if I had come from Russia he would employ me. I had come from England so I had no chance. He knew that in England there had been a political training camp. As he had no way of knowing who had been at this camp then he just said to everyone what came from there that was his reason. One day a girl from the local labor office came to me and gave me a work order to go and work in a nearby forest. My father said this was no good work. I did not go. Where they got my name from I do not know. I had not registered there yet, as I had in mind going back to the west. I had kept in touch with my sister and she told me she would leave quite soon as well.

Chapter Fifteen: Crossing the Border

I had got to know a family in the village who went to the west, quite often, illegally. One day I joined up with a girl and crossed over with her. I did stay only a few days. I just wanted to know the way. This crossing proved very valuable to me later on. I traveled with the girl to my sister Lotte in the town near the border. We stopped over at the N.K.W.D. house as it was the safest place in town. Besides, it was on the way to the border 6 KM away. After midnight about 2am we got up. My sister made sure that all was clear and I left with the girl. This crossing was the easiest I experienced. We crossed over by daylight and took the streetcar to Lubeck. A few days later I went back. It was just impossible to find a place to stay in the city. Not even a little room. As soon as I was back my sister said she was ready to go and asked if I could guide her over. It was the only time this would work as I still had some money which I received in Hamburg. She was never able to go before as she had no Western money and I having some was just what she needed to go over. One afternoon I went to her again in the same N.K.W.D. house. All was quiet. We left the house after midnight and as soon as we were 100 metres away I turned off the street and we went across the field from then on.

It took about 1 ½ hrs. to come close to the border. The first fields were quite open, then some bush after that a field again. The field ended on a farming road and on the other side of that was the west. The first part was uneventful, just a few fences to cross, and in the bush the owls hooting at night would give you a scare. On crossing the border there was one rule: keep walking and keep your senses working. We had just come out of the bush entered the field and I smelled cigarette smoke. I pulled my sister down and in a flash we were not able to see anybody. We kept still and then we heard muffled voices. It was 2 men in a shallow ditch. They had stopped there for a smoke. It was rather careless. We did not waste time with them as the border was only 400 metres to go. It was the last stretch across the field to the road. Time was in the middle of the hour so the guard would have passed this point by now. I got my sister to the road showed her were to go and she went across. I waited for a while. As I heard nothing I started my way back. Sometime later, I would be back at this same point but under much different circumstances. By the time I reached town it was daybreak. I passed the N.K.W.D. house and had a smile because I knew they would have no breakfast this morning. By noon I was home and could tell my parents that it had worked out all right. Within a week we had mail. Lotte was already working in Düsseldorf.

She thanked me for the money as it made things a lot easier. It was only 40 marks, but it was a start. In the village the labor office was still after me. On my walks through the village I had seen some posters. The Wismuth complex was looking for workers in Uranium mines near the Czechoslovakia border. The posters gave terrific wages 350 marks a month and more. Even 250 marks was a lot. On the other side, the talk about this complex was positive. I asked the labor office for a pass to the mines which I got quite easily. They were glad to have somebody for Aue as it was called. It took a day and ½ to get there. Here the land was so much higher and in the middle of April was still snow on the ground. In Aue I had a medical and the doctor made it quite clear this was the last chance to get out. I was with others and nobody refused because where we came from was no work and the labor office at home would certainly be notified of your decision. So everyone signed up. At once our J.D. cards were collected and we got new ones from the Wismuth A.G. firm. I got detailed to a complex of 5 mines and the 75 living quarters were 2 miles off in a village. This building for our quarters had been a sponge factory before the war. It had big rooms which were divided to hold about 20 men. Bedding was supplied. In the building was a kitchen, which had a big stove and who ever had something to eat made it at on the stove.

Everyone received a coupon after end of the work shift for a hot meal in a commercial kitchen. It was a good meal, the only drawback was it was not on the way home. The town I was in was quite hilly and you seemed to walk for ever uphill. Work was around the clock 3 shifts and on Sundays you volunteered for a shift in honor of Comrade Stalin or in honor of the Russian-German friendship committee who were on a visit in Moscow. Every Sunday somebody else got honored by our work. In the mine I worked in, I was with 5 others and it was called a brigade. The work we did was go down deeper as other brigades went horizontal. The sink, as our place was called, was not liked much by anybody. It rained constantly and the protective clothing we had was good for one hour. We had to drill about 6 feet into hard rock. Usually we drilled 28 holes in a square of about 12 by 15 feet. After the drilling the shooter came, loaded the holes and blasted it out. After the blasting we were supposed to wait for the air to clear. While you waited you made no progress. Our Brigadier usually went in after 20 minutes with the place still full of gases. For a while I did not go in right away. The point was to go down a least 4-5 feet a shift. Good blasting would give you 6 feet once or twice a shift. The Steiger would come and measure our progress. Also, every so often, a Russian soldier would show up who was very likely an engineer in mining. The first month was not a full month and I got no extra pay for fulfilling the norm. One day in the mine the power went out for 6 hours. The norm for the month was already gone. The electricians could not find the trouble. In the end, the main switch was found in the off position. The cry was sabotage.

What the norm was we never found out. One month we made 27 meters down and the other brigade we were told had made 28 meters and they received the flag for good work. Our Brigadier knew he could make 28 meters next month. He made 29. He did not get the flag, but a coupon to buy a bicycle. It was about as useless as roller-skates because the country was just so hilly for bicycles. On the other hand if you had a bike in town you were looked upon as a good worker. Everything was worn. I hated to go down the mine on the 2 pm shift because the sun was shining and you went down 300-400 meters. By 10 pm it was dark when you came out. Sometimes while we waited upstairs we could hear the blasting from below. We knew it would be hard work right on entering.

One month no brigade below ground had fulfilled the norm. We were told we had worked 29 days in the month where it should have been 25 days. We claimed we had worked in honor of Comrade Stalin and the month should be donated for 25 days. This would give us our norm and slightly better, but our protest was no good. We were asked if we wanted to shoot Comrade Stalin. Who could argue with such a good reason as nobody had the norm underground but the mine had to have some quota fulfilled. The surveyors above ground were the lucky ones. We could not figure this out. They could only measure what we had done and we had done the norm. What could you do? The only right you had was to work. You could not leave as you had no I.D. Card.

While I was in Aue the government prepared for elections. If I wanted to vote or not we were marched to a meeting hall and had to listen to a speaker and some committee which in my way of thinking twisted everything around. In the end everyone applauded as you dared not to. One Sunday was the election. I had come off my shift at 6 am and by the time I got to sleep it was close to 9 am. At 10 I was awakened by a lot of noise. Outside was a band also some flags and a speaker informed us Mine 72 had already voted 100% and we were still in competition with another mine and we could beat them by marching to the polling station right now. What could we do? We lined up and were marched with music and big notices which read Mine 75 votes 100% Yes for the S.E.D. How did they know before the election. I did not vote yes. It did you no good to go behind a curtain to mark your ballet. A good Communist voted in the open on the table in front of everyone. You had nothing to hide. All the parties were the same anyway and all represented Communism.

We had a library in the building. I found some books which interested me. I read one of Stalin's speeches during the war. I was curious to find out how he had faced the war. It was quite interesting. The book was a good choice as it saved me a lot later.

One afternoon I had just got up. My bed was still not made, but the book was there on top. I was on the far wall away from the door and I had just dressed and through the door came a Russian officer. More men were in the room and before he got to me he could have stopped and talked to any one of them. He did not he know exactly where my bed was, which shift I was on, and that I was awake. I thought this over later after I heard from others about who this officer was and I came to the conclusion that there was a good informer in the room. The officer sat down not on my bed, but he pulled a chair up. He spoke good German. He made some small talk about work so what could I say. I praised the work. He gave me hell for having my sheets in such a mess. The bed was not made. He noticed the book, looked at the title and apparently he liked what I read. He asked me about it. I claimed Stalin was a great comrade during the war. He left quite friendly. I hated him for lecturing me on my unmade bed. In Russia, he probably had no sheets at all. After he had gone the man next to me asked me if I knew who that officer was. I did not. He knew. It was a Russian Intelligence Officer. About this time, my papers must have been in his office. As a prisoner from England he must have seen reason to look me over. I am sure he gave me a good report. I had Stalin's book on my bed. Whatever report he gave me after his visit, it very likely sent him to Siberia because 2 weeks later I was in the west.

His visit got me thinking. I did not look for the informer in the room. I was always exhausted after my shift. I liked the fresh air and I hated going below ground. I had a workers' pass for the railway and for about 20 marks I could go home. I did this quite often. The labor office in the village was quite proud of me whenever I was home. It showed it was good in Aue. My reason for going home was to keep in touch with the family who crossed the border at times and they kept me up to date on the guards.

One day I was in the mine and the bucket came down to fill with rock the bucket which weighed a ton. Quite big and I tried to move it the handle came down and broke my finger. I went up to the next level to get out. Here I found that the lift to the top did

the worst you could do to the German Democratic Republic. Near Berlin I got off. It was rush hour. I boarded a streetcar which I know would bring me to the west. What I did not know was that there was a pass control station before you crossed to the West Sector. The streetcar was loaded. To my luck 2 Volkspolice came through and just glanced at papers. I had my Wismuth pass on hand they must have thought it was a Western Pass. I cleared. In Berlin I looked up the woman I had written to from England and who had notified my parents at that time. I was looking for a flight out, it would have been the safest for me. The only drawback was a waiting time of 6 weeks in a camp. I was not going to wait that long.

I stopped over in Berlin for a few days and I found conditions for flights out did not change. Once as I walked along a Berlin street, I was invited by a tourist guide to come and visit on the other side of the Brandenburg Gate. I would have liked to but I did not dare leaving the west sector. That same afternoon I was run into by a man in a little store. I thought nothing of it. He apologized. I found out later the only ID card I had was missing. I had it in the coat pocket. What he got wasn't much by now as did not care if I had an Identification Card or not. The next day I booked a train in Berlin to the Baltic Sea. My ticket destination was not close to the border, I obtained that later. I changed trains one morning and made the last trip to the border. The train station was only 10 km from home. I did not go home as I did not want my parents involved in my escape. I was at the station early in the afternoon. I left at once with the other passengers as anyone carrying a suitcase at train time was quite safe walking a short distance. I passed the house of the N.K.W.D again. I had just crossed the bridge when a girl waved to me to take cover, but it was too late for that. I just turned in time and I walked towards town and not the border. What came at me was a truckload of Volkspolice. They had no reason to stop me because I was walking towards town. As soon as they were out of sight I turned again. I spotted some bushes on the rail line and I decided to wait here till dark.

I had not been in the bushes long when I looked up. I looked right at a German Shepherd dog no more than 5 feet away. I was eating and he must have smelled something from the road on the embankment. I did not know what to do. I wasted no time with the dog. I was able to tease the dog away. This incident taught me the lesson never to hide to close to a road where you had only one open view. I knew I had quite a few hours to wait here so I settled down a bit further off. By about 10 pm I moved out again as I had earlier with my sister across fields. It was summer now. I came across one meadow where the cows were out. Soon as they saw me they all started walking towards me. I surely did not need cows to give me away now as I only had 1 ½ KM to the border. If anybody was watching the herd it would be just my luck he would have seen me. I went to the ground and let the cows calm down. They thought I was going to feed them. Coming near the bush, I heard owls again. No smokers at the ditch this time. It had become harder to cross over. People talked a lot about it in the village and lots of people left as they could see soon it would be impossible to cross. They were right. Positioning myself at the ditch I looked at the field for the last 400 metres. I waited here a long time. I studied the field well. I could see a path leading to the road which marked the border.

At the end of the path were some bushes, on the edge of the field, and then the road. When I finally started walking my mind was made up, I would cross no matter what or who tried to stop me. To be like this was a pity. You could not even walk in your own country where ever you wanted to. I started to walk, but did not follow the path. I was about 30 meters to the left of it in the wheat. I went quite low and just cleared the top. I found what would save me. I gentle wind was blowing this night. It came towards me. When I had reached the hedge on the other end of the field I found I had come out close to the end of the path and the end of the bushes. I moved right away from this spot. I could see the West now even in the dark. All I had to do was to cross the farming road and the field on the other side. It was open, but once across the road, it was just a matter of how fast one could run for 200 metres. Just to be away from the road a little distance to the west made you safe. The fact was that once you had cleared the road you did not stop running for quite a distance. While I was in bushes now I had time to look things over. I decided not to cross right away. I found that later I might have made it. I looked at my watch, it was ¼ to the full hour. I knew if the guard came by it would not be long because his station was just up the road a short distance. He would very likely change on the full hour. I had just settled in the bushes near the road when the wind brought some noises towards me.

I could hear someone walking in heavy boots. I did not move, but I could see 2 Volkspolice with a dog on a leash. This was what I had heard. They stopped and I could clearly hear them say that nobody was coming tonight. They stopped and looked at the path with binoculars. They were right nobody was coming even though I was right under their nose, the dog was not very active and it did not smell me out as the wind was in my favor. When they walked away they passed me by less than 10 feet. After this I knew I would make it. But I waited for another 15 minutes and then I just ran across as fast as I could. If I had crossed right after I had arrived at the road the dog would have seen me and caught up with me on the ploughed field. At the end of the field I found a furrow were I lay down and looked back. I did not feel sorry at all because I hated everything the East stood for and represented. After a little while, I started to walk towards a street I knew was not far. This street I used quite freely once I was on it. After a short walk I came upon 2 policemen from the west. I walked up to this and told them I had just crossed over. They advised me to go to a camp some 15 KM away so I walked. They said it was a long walk. Not for me. I was free and quite happy to walk 15 KM that night.

I have not been back to the East to this day, 29 years later as I write this. Just a few months in the East had given me enough reason to stay away for a life time from all that represents Communism.

I found the camp that the policeman had told me about quite easily. I arrived early in the morning. It was not crowded. A lot of young people. The older ones very likely could not stand the strain of crossing here. It was easier for them to go to Berlin and fly out. The formalities at the reception camp did not take long and I was able to get a letter off to my sister in Dusseldorf that very same day. She had expected me, but not so soon. After she had left, it was only a few months in between. She sent me some money and I was quite well off in this camp. After about 3 days I was interviewed by an Englishman as it was the English zone and I had no problem to convince him that I had to stay in the West. He asked for my pass from the Uranium mines, but I did not have it any more. However, I gave him the location of the mine, which he could find easily enough. After that I was asked where I wanted to settle in the West. I chose the Rhineland not too far from Dusseldorf. As it turned out I was about 50 Kilometers away after I had my railway pass. I was supposed to report to a farmer. I did so it was near Cologne. I told the farmer right away I would not stay long. He had one other helper and this man convinced me to stay on as the work was good for this farmer. What I had seen in the first few hours I did not like much. They were good Catholics and it clashed with my behavior.

The next morning after breakfast I left. I was on my way to Dusseldorf. I made the city by night fall and stopped over in a house run by monks. They gave me food for a day and a ticket to get back into the city as it was some ways off for Dusseldorf. I walked along the Konigsallee like a real tramp. I had no idea this was the showcase of the west. The street where my sister was not far away. I went through the park on the Rhine and here I ran into my sister. From here on it went easy for me. She showed me the employment office and I was working that same day on a farm just outside of Düsseldorf.

The next Sunday I went to see my sister again and things were quite normal with us. We both didn't have much money but we had found a place to stay and got paid every week. It could only get better for us both. Sundays when we were out on the Rhine she spent 3 marks for coffee and cake one time. I thought that was an awful lot of money. I made 15 marks a week and I had free board and lodging. Later, when I was feeding the horses it was up to 18 marks. I stayed with the farmer all summer and fall of the year 1949. I liked the work and the easy way to get to town. In the late fall another man came to the farm from the East. He was just looking for shelter. He found me a room too. I left the farmer and started to work on a construction site as a helper for a bricklayer. My pay now was 60 marks, but 30 I had to pay for food and lodging. However, it was still good. Before Christmas, construction closed down.

I had always had a ride on the streetcar. I wondered one day about working on the streetcars. The next day I was hired started with the Rheinbahn (Rhine Train) January 2 1950. The year 1949 had been a rather turbulent one. From 1950 onwards things went better. The pay was good and as soon as my 3 weeks training was over I knew where I would be. I put an ad in the paper. Young man clean job wants room. I had a letter from Urdenbach. I thought was a bit off my way. As I had free travel on the streetcar I went to see the place. I liked it and rented it right away. While I had been with the farmer I had been in Urdenbach once for some hay. I did not remember much from the drive through with the wagon. One time while coming home from the field I looked at the people on the sidewalk and there was one I knew. It was an old P.O.W. from England in the officer's mess. He knew the farms around here and visited me next evening. I still write to him after all these years. We still exchange yarns from the officers mess. How could we forget that the people in Urdenbach were real nice. I bought a bike there for 120 marks in the next town one mile away. It was really good and it served me for 4 years.

I visited Lotte my sister quite regularly. One time at carnival she had tickets for a big ball. We were new to this. We had no idea what was going on. Everyone had a bottle of wine. We had no money. She went home as it was only around the corner and got some so we also had a bottle of wine. She told me at times she had met some other people but not much. One day I was with her on a Sunday. She said I know a very rich man now and I think he means business with marriage. I told her right away to go ahead. Four weeks later I was the best man at the wedding. My sister became Mrs. Hasemann. She had hardly any clothes and no bedding so for the present I gave her bed sheets which she needed. At least she had something when she moved

Rheinbahn Düsseldorf 1950-54
RHEIN BAHN
6.1.1950.
6.8.1953.
1950
1951
1951
Die Fahrkarten „Bitte"
1953
1951

Both pages: photos from Manfred's days in Hamburg. (Roy Gutzke Collection)

in. She was not mistaken. The man was very good to her. He had a car, a good income and they hit it off real nice. So the year 1950 onwards really changed things for us. I was still with the Rheinbahn but had changed to buses. It was closer to the depot where I had to go to work. It was just one mile. I liked it. Sure it was shift work but it was clean, paid good and you were always in the shadow of the excitement of a big city. Düsseldorf was being rebuilt. The work was going on 7 days a week, some buildings around the clock everything was going full blast. But every so often you were reminded of the past. A bomb was found while clearing a building site. All streetcars were rerouted at times, but the fire workers always managed to defuse the heavy ones. One time in 1953 I heard that one of our bus operators had left and gone to Canada. He went to Toronto. I thought nothing of it, but kept it in my mind. By 1954 I knew I would go to Canada. My mind was made up.

Epilogue

Anyone who has lived through a war and survived it like the Second World War in Europe can tell you what a defeated nation looks like and will tell you what total Military occupation is like. The victorious Military rules as a civilization in your country your rights are Military law. Whatever the Victors want to do, they do. As long as the fighting is on, any woman is fair game to be raped over and over. Anything the troops or soldiers fancy is theirs, be it from a home or a state owned building. Anything from a museum a soldier wants is gone. There is absolutely nothing a defeated nation can do about it. Good houses that the occupation forces want, the Military will take and the owner has 24 hours to move out and leave all furniture in the house. If he has no place to go to that is too bad who cares such as it was in Germany in 1945 – most all cities were at least ¾ bombed out. What was left was not enough to live in and have shelter. Anything good was for officers of the victorious nations. Industrial plants of any value got dismantled shipped to whoever wanted them. They went mostly to Russia.

In 1945 the very large forest in the Harz Mountains were located in the British zone and for some reason England needed lumber, so the Germans had to cut down half of their Harz forest and ship all the lumber to England because Military Rule said so. Anything they wanted was taken. Objections were no good. You had lost the war and had to pay for it. Because Germany had started it in 1939, the defeat was total. Revenge by the victors at that time was sweet. If there was any production in factories that the population could use it was not for locals, everything belonged to the victors. New homes had to be built for occupation forces, even though lots of local people were living in cellars, which was better than in the open in a lean to. It took years before Germany had anything resembling a normal living standard. Ration cards were still in use in 1948. Ration cards started Sept 1 1939 it was said on a temporary basis. At wars end, money was of no value. War decorations worn by soldiers were sought by the occupation troops for cigarettes from Iron Cross 2nd Class: 20 cigarettes; 1st Class: 40 or more.

Higher or rarer decorations for valor brought more cigarettes in return and bought everything from food to clothes and old cars. It was often said in Germany "Enjoy the war., the peace will be terrible". Those words were truly spoken because everybody only cared about himself and that was more than enough. Nobody knew what tomorrow would bring. If you had a job working for the occupation army and you got some food at times you considered yourself lucky. Unless you have lived through such a period, not even your imagination could visualize this.

My parents home was in the eastern part of Germany and East of the Oder River. Our city Belgard had no war manufacture industry. All the land around was agricultural. As the war went on we heard on the radio and by word of mouth the Royal Air Force was bombing the cities in the west mainly the one's with war production. We heard it, but paid little attention to it. It was far away. The bombed out people as much as possible were relocated to the East. Not too many though as this would have given away the extent of the bombing.

By the end of 1944 we had to take in a bombed out family in our house. It was okay as everybody had to take in somebody. We were glad we did not get bombed. Whatever should happen to us in the east of Germany was far worse than the bombs in the west. By wars end, the Red Army had overrun all of the east and middle Germany. Women had to endure a lot. Men were rounded up in every village and never heard from again. From our village 17 were missing. Then the Poles came as all the parts east of the Oder River was given to Poland. They came in horse drawn wagons went up and down the street looking for a house to take over. If they found what they liked, they went to the Melize (Polish Police) told them what they wanted to take over. The Melize would inform the German owner he had 20 minutes to get out with 30 pounds of luggage. There was no pleading or begging to stay, it was 20 minutes or get shot. It was very simple, the Germans had started and lost the war so they had to be punished. While some in the west thought the bombing was bad, this, to be chased from your own house and home with 30 pounds of luggage, was far worse. It did you no good to take anything valuable before you left your house because the Polish people searched you and took what they figured was of value from you. If you had good shoes on, you turned them over and you walked barefoot.

This part of Germany had been German for 800 years. It was the English Prime Minister Churchill who found that part of Germany had been Polish a 1000 years ago and Poles supported by the Red Army who had overrun this part of Germany was called the Polish Liberation Army so that was that. My father was soldiering in the West. My mother and 2 sisters had managed through the efforts of my older sister to flee about a week before the Polish Liberation Army came in. As we later heard from some, who were not able to get out before, that the Russian

Commandant was looking for our family. There were some left in the village who tried to be friendly with the Poles and would help them in some way by talking to them about the people in the village they had lived and grown up with. As a kid I had a 22 rifle so when the Poles came in I was the villain with the rifle.

Many people from the east found each other again in the West years later. From the ones who had talked and had given others away, nothing was ever heard from them again. It is possible they knew they had done wrong and did not want to be found by their old village friends as they once were. One family was always known as Communists in the village. As soon as the Red Army found out they were shot. The Germans became each other's worst enemies.

After lots of turmoil in Germany in the 1920's and early 1930's, Hitler and his party was chosen to rule Germany as of January 30, 1933. He called it the third Reich and said it would last for 1000 years. In March 1933, there were elections in Germany. Hitler's party had not gained a majority but it was the strongest over all the splinter parties. in 1933, he created the "Ermechtigungs Gesetz" (the full power law). March of 1933 was the last time that Germans would see free elections until 1946. Hitler's 1000 year Reich lasted 12 years, 3 months and 10 days in a way. Some might say, and rightly so, that it was only 10 years and 3 days, since on the 2nd of February 1943, the German 6th Army surrendered at Stalingrad. This was in a way a Victory for the Red Army but the German "Wehrmacht" was still a formidable fighting force. The victory was to go to either Nazis or Communists and the communists won. The battle of Kursk in Russia in 1943 saw the defeat of the Wehrmacht at the hands of the Red Army. After the battle of Kursk, the Red Army dictated where and when to fight in the East and the Wehrmact never again started any offensive. It fell back out of Russia and

Poland to the river Elbe. That marked the end of a once proud army, beaten and defeated in the worst way. It was the first time in modern history that an entire armed forces of a country surrendered and became prisoners of war.

Up to 1939, a lot of the Polish army had escaped. Up to 1940, it was the same for France. However, up to 1945 no one escaped from the German armed forces .

By 1936, the thinking in Germany was like this. When the Nazi's came and took the Communists away, I did not protest because I was not a communist. When they came and took the Jews away, I did not protest because I was not a Jew. When they took the Jehova's Witnesses away, I did not protest because I was not one of them either. When they came and took me away, there was no one left to protest.

At that time, it was best to walk quietly and say nothing, If you went to church on Sundays, the priest included Hitler in his blessings. If he did not do so, he would not be a priest much longer. It would be said that he would be transferred to another region, location unknown.

Forty-two years later, 1987, my sister had made a visit to our home village as relations between Germany and Poland had become friendlier. She was allowed in the house that my father had built in 1926-27 and now belonged after 1945 to the Poles. Even some of our furniture was still there. The Poles, as they told her, had to buy the house from the Polish Government. The first few years after the war they were always afraid the Germans would come back. This fear eased over the years and has now disappeared in Poland. My sister advised me never to visit this place again as it was not as we knew it and she was quite happy where she was now in the West and so was I in Canada.

Left: the author happy to be in Canada.

Above: Manfred and his sister in later years at a market. Manfred's son Roy is to his left.

Above: Manfred's wife, Gerda Gutzke.

About the Author

Manfred emigrated to Canada in the early 1950s. He met his wife, Gerda, in Toronto. She was also from Germany. Gerda had been in Liepzig during the war. After the war, Gerda struggled to escape from the Russian Zone of Eastern Germany. She swam across canals, scaled fences, and was even caught once before she eventually escaped and wound up in Toronto. Manfred and Gerda had a long and successful marriage.

Manfred's first job was as a gas station attendant in the Rosedale area of Toronto. Later, he worked as a prison guard at the infamous Don Jail. During his time working at the jail, he had interactions with the famous Toronto bank robber "Edwin Alonso Boyd" of the Boyd Gang, who was imprisoned there during Manfred's brief 1 year tenure at the jail. After that Manfred became a police officer at the Woodbine race track in Etobicoke (and occasionally other Ontario racetracks). During this time, there was a royal visit and he actually got to escort Queen Elizabeth in an elevator. After this, Manfred had a long run in the billing department of Shell Oil at the Don Mills Data Centre (which no longer exists). He finished his working career there after 24 years of service. Manfred was active with gardening and handicrafts until his passing.

Related Books by Travelogue 219:
www.tl219.com

A Token Force: *The 261st Field Park Company Royal Engineers (Airborne) at Arnhem* by John Sliz
ISBN: 978-0-9877404-6-5

Basic Function: *The 4th Parachute Squadron, Royal Engineers at Arnhem* by John Sliz
ISBN: 978-0-9783838-1-7

Bridging the Club Route: *Guards Armoured Division's Engineers During Operation Market Garden* by John Sliz
ISBN: 978-1-927679-14-2

Churchill's Warriors: *Personal Stories of British Airborne Troops in the Second World War* by Andy Johnston
ISBN: 978-1-927679-63-0

Commander Royal Engineers: *The Headquarters of the Royal Engineers at Arnhem* by John Sliz
ISBN: 978-1-92679-04-3

Engineers at the Bridge: *The 1st Parachute Squadron Royal Engineers at Arnhem* by John Sliz
ISBN: 978-0-9783838-4-8

Gales' Eyes Part I: *Headquarters and the Brigades*
by Carl Rymen
ISBN 978-1-927679-50-0

Gales' Eyes Part II: *Support Units*
by Carl Rymen
ISBN 978-1-927679-62-3

Officers at Arnhem *An Examination of the Command Structure of the British 1st Airborne Division Which Fought at Arnhem in September **1944***
by Trevor Laing
ISBN: 978-1-927679-27-2

The Wrong Side of the River: *The Polish Engineer Company at Arnhem* by John Sliz
ISBN: 978-09783838-0-0

Made in the USA
Middletown, DE
06 March 2018